Favorite
Food at Home

Favorite
Food at Home

Delicious Comfort Food from Ireland's
Most Famous Chef

Rachel Allen

WILLIAM MORROW
An Imprint of HarperCollins*Publishers*

I dedicate this book to my husband, Isaac, whose love,
wisdom and inspiration I could not live without

This book was first published in Great Britain in 2006 by Collins, an imprint of
HarperCollins Publishers Ltd.

HarperCollins books may be purchased for educational, business, or sales promotional
use. For information please write: Special Markets Department, HarperCollins Publishers,
10 East 53rd Street, New York, NY 10022.

FIRST U.S. EDITION

Library of Congress Cataloging-in Publication Data has been applied for.

ISBN 978-0-06-180927-9

10   11   12   13   14   [LEO]   10   9   8   7   6   5   4   3   2   1

Contents

Introduction 9

1 Easy Family Food 11

2 Sweet Celebrations 35

3 Picnics and Days Out 53

4 Food for Children 71

5 Extended Family 93

6 Dining Alfresco 115

7 Home Cinema 135

8 Big Celebrations 149

9 Edible Gifts 173

10 Just Like Mum Used to Make 195

Useful Extras 213

Index 222

Acknowledgments 224

Introduction

I think my very earliest memory of food (actually, probably my earliest memory of anything) is of my sister, Simone, feeding me mashed banana as though I were her baby. She's four years older than me and as she was probably only about five or six at the time, I was only about two! Then, when we were a bit older, we loved helping Mum in the kitchen (although now I can imagine that we were probably not that much help), and would often bake cakes and biscuits ourselves. We were very lucky that there was always good home-cooked food in the house, even when Mum was working, and we always sat down at the table together as a family and enjoyed great chats. Often there would be friends there too. It is still the same when I stay with my parents in Dublin.

So now that I have children myself, cooking at home is very important to me. It evokes such happy childhood memories. I also love that time of the evening when my husband, Isaac, gets home from work and we have a glass of wine in the kitchen while one of us prepares supper. This is our time for catching up on what's been going on during the day. Of course, there is the added pleasure of our children's company – even if they are fighting!

Many of you may be parents, and working ones at that, so I have included plenty of suggestions in this book for easy meals that all the family can enjoy. Even better, they can be whipped up in no time. But there is so much more to enjoying cooking at home, like those times when you are looking forward to friends or family coming to stay, or when you're planning a big party for a special occasion, or when it's such a glorious day that you decide to have a spontaneous lunchtime barbecue or a little alfresco dinner party on a balmy evening. There are also those important times when only Mum's cooking will do—I know that's how I feel about my own mum's food, and hopefully my children will feel the same about mine. You may want to bake a gorgeous cake or some buns for that special somebody on a special day, or even make completely delicious edible gifts. Cooking great food at home is a joy that I wish to pass along to you. Among the many recipes in this book I hope there is inspiration aplenty, and that this book will become a much-loved member of your family. May it last you many happy years, and feed you many joyous meals!

1 Easy Family Food

I love family meals since this is when everyone gets to sit together and talk about what went on during the day. This type of food should be easy to prepare and quick to rustle up, or else made in advance earlier in the day. This is simple food that the whole family will enjoy and the recipes can be easily amended to suit everyone's taste.

Scrambled Eggs with Tomato, Chile and Cilantro

SERVES 2 / VEGETARIAN

I love this scrambled egg variation, which I first tasted in a restaurant looking out over Mexico City. It's full of protein (from the eggs) and antioxidants (from the cilantro), and is a great way to start the day. Of course, you can omit the chile for children; the cilantro still makes it special.

1 tbsp butter
1 ripe tomato, finely chopped
½–1 chile, deseeded and finely chopped (optional for children)
4 free-range eggs, best quality possible
3 tbsp milk
Salt and freshly ground black pepper
1 tbsp chopped fresh cilantro

Melt the butter in a saucepan, add the tomato and chile and cook for a few minutes until the tomato is just softening. Meanwhile, whisk the eggs with the milk and a pinch of salt and pepper. Add to the saucepan and stir gently until the egg is softly scrambled. Stir in the chopped cilantro and serve.

Berry Breakfast Muffins

MAKES 12 / VEGETARIAN

These are gorgeous muffins and they make delicious breakfast fare. The best thing about this basic recipe is that you can add whatever fruit you like.

2 eggs
6 tbsp milk
6 tbsp plain yogurt
1/3 c sunflower oil
1 tsp vanilla extract
1/2 lb berries, such as raspberries,
    blueberries or blackberries
1 3/4 c (8 oz) all-purpose flour

1 tbsp baking powder
1/4 tsp baking soda
1/4 tsp salt
1/2 tsp ground cinnamon
1 c (4 oz) whole wheat flour
1/2 c (4 oz) light brown sugar, plus
    1-2 tbsp for sprinkling (optional)

Preheat the oven to 350°F (180°C). Line a muffin pan with 12 paper muffin cups. Break the eggs into a large mixing bowl and whisk to break up. Whisk in the milk, yogurt, oil and vanilla. Add the berries and stir.

In another bowl sift the all-purpose flour, baking powder, baking soda, salt and cinnamon. Add the whole wheat flour and sugar, and mix. Fold the dry ingredients into the wet ingredients. Stop mixing as soon as it comes together; do not overstir.

Divide the mixture between the muffin cups, sprinkle the tops with brown sugar, if using, and cook in the preheated oven for 20-25 minutes, or until the tops spring back when gently touched. Allow to stand in the pan for 1-2 minutes, then transfer to a wire rack to cool.

RACHEL'S HANDY TIP
If your children won't eat a whole muffin, you can make these in a mini-muffin pan. If you halve the recipe, you will get 12 mini-muffins. Bake for 12-15 minutes.

VARIATIONS
PEACH OR PEACH AND BANANA MUFFINS
Use 2 peaches that have been pitted and chopped into 1/4-1/2-inch cubes after you have whisked in the milk, yogurt, oil and vanilla. For yet more variety replace half the chopped peach with one mashed banana.

APPLE AND CINNAMON MUFFINS

These are so yummy; a cooking apple works better than a plain eating apple. Use 1/2 lb grated, unpeeled cooking apple as for the peach variation.

RHUBARB AND GINGER MUFFINS

These are great as you can use frozen rhubarb. Use 1/2 lb trimmed, finely chopped (1/4-inch pieces) rhubarb in place of the peach, plus 1 generous teaspoon finely grated ginger (whisked in with the wet ingredients).

Chicken, Ginger and Cashew Stir-fry with Coconut Noodles

SERVES 4-6

This delicious and easy stir-fry is very quick to prepare for both friends and family; it is a favorite of ours and makes a yummy and healthy supper. If you do not have a wok, use a large, heavy-bottomed frying pan.

FOR THE NOODLES:
$4^{1}/_{4}$ c vegetable (or chicken) stock
One $13^{1}/_{2}$-oz can coconut milk
1 lb thin egg noodles

FOR THE STIR-FRY:
2 tbsp sesame oil
1 tbsp sunflower oil
6 large garlic cloves, peeled and finely chopped
1 tbsp finely grated ginger

1 lb chicken breasts, cut into thin strips
1 carrot, peeled, cut in half lengthwise and very thinly sliced at an angle
5 oz snow peas, cut in half at an angle
9 oz mushrooms, sliced
5 oz unsalted cashew nuts or peanuts, toasted and roughly chopped
3 tbsp chopped fresh cilantro
Salt and freshly ground black pepper

First, prepare the coconut noodles. Place the stock and coconut milk in a saucepan and bring to the boil. Add the noodles and cook according to the instructions on the package. When cooked, drain. To prevent them from sticking together, add a couple of tablespoonfuls of the cooking liquid to the noodles. Cover and keep warm.

Meanwhile, heat a wok until almost smoking, add the sesame and sunflower oils and the garlic and ginger. Cook for a few seconds, then add the chicken and cook for a few minutes, stirring regularly, until the outside is just golden. Add the carrots, snow peas and mushrooms, then toss and stir for another few minutes until the vegetables are just cooked but still slightly crunchy. Toss in the nuts and chopped cilantro and season. Serve on top of the noodles.

Broccoli Soup with Parmesan Toasts

SERVES 6-8 / VEGETARIAN

I adore this delicious and nutritious soup. It's great either for family suppers or for a dinner party. The soup can be frozen and the Parmesan toasts prepared in advance, then grilled at the last moment. Ideal if you need a meal in an instant.

FOR THE SOUP:
2 tbsp butter
2 potatoes, peeled and finely chopped
1 large onion, peeled and chopped
Salt and freshly ground black pepper
1 head of broccoli, with stalk
$3^1/_2$-$4^1/_4$ c hot vegetable (or chicken) stock
3/4 c heavy cream
FOR THE PARMESAN TOASTS:
8 slices good-quality white bread
3 oz Parmesan cheese, finely grated

Melt the butter in a medium to large saucepan, and add the potatoes and onion, salt and pepper. Cover with a piece of wax paper and sweat over a gentle heat for 10 minutes.

Meanwhile, cut the broccoli florets from the stalk. Using a small knife, remove the outer layer of skin from the stalk and discard, then chop the stalk into $1/_2$-inch pieces. Add to the onion and potato, cover and sweat for a further 5 minutes.

Add the hot stock to the potatoes, onion and broccoli stalk, bring up to the boil, then add the chopped florets. Boil without the lid over a high heat for 4-5 minutes until soft, then add the cream. Remove from the heat, puree in a blender and season to taste.

To make the Parmesan toasts, toast the bread on both sides, sprinkle with grated Parmesan and pop under a hot grill or into a hot oven for 2 minutes or until the cheese melts. Cut the toast into fingers and serve on the side with the soup.

Risotto Verde

SERVES 6 / VEGETARIAN

This is a gorgeous, fresh tasting green risotto and is easy to make as it is baked in the oven.

4 tbsp olive oil
10 oz green peas (fresh or frozen)
4 oz spinach, destalked and chopped
4 c vegetable (or chicken) stock
1 onion, peeled and finely chopped
2 garlic cloves, peeled and crushed
Salt and freshly ground black pepper
12 oz risotto rice, such as arborio or carnaroli
2/3 c white wine
12 stalks of asparagus, ends trimmed and cut in half lengthwise
4 oz Parmesan cheese, shaved, to serve

Preheat the oven to 350°F (180°C). On the stove top, heat half the olive oil in an ovenproof saucepan, add the peas and spinach and cook, stirring all the time, for 2 minutes, until the spinach wilts. Add about 1/4 c of the stock and puree in a blender or food processor. Set aside.

In the same saucepan, heat the remaining olive oil, add the onion and garlic and season with salt and pepper. Cover with a lid and sweat over a gentle heat until soft but not colored. Add the risotto rice and stir it around in the saucepan for a minute, then add the remaining stock and the wine. Stir and bring it up to the boil, cover with the lid and place in the preheated oven for 15–20 minutes or until the rice is just cooked and all the liquid has been absorbed. Stir in the vegetable puree and set aside with the lid on.

Bring a saucepan of water up to the boil, add a good pinch of salt and the asparagus. Boil for 2–3 minutes or until it is just tender, then drain. Serve the risotto in warm bowls with the asparagus and Parmesan arranged on top.

RACHEL'S HANDY TIP
The alcohol in the wine burns off during cooking and the flavor is lovely, but if you do not want to use it, just replace it with extra stock.

Pasta with Spinach, Bacon and Parmesan
SERVES 4

This is a delicious and super-quick recipe. A firm family favorite!

14 oz spaghetti or tagliatelle
2 tbsp olive oil
¼ lb sliced bacon, chopped
2-3 garlic cloves, peeled and finely chopped
5 oz baby spinach leaves
Salt and freshly ground black pepper
2 oz Parmesan cheese, or something similar, freshly grated, to serve

Put a large saucepan of water on to boil and add 1 teaspoon salt. When boiling, add the pasta, stir well and cook rapidly until al dente.

While the pasta is cooking, heat the oil in a large frying pan, add the bacon and garlic and cook on a high heat for about 4 minutes until the bacon is golden and slightly crispy. Add the spinach and stir until it has wilted. Season to taste.

Drain the pasta when cooked and return to the large saucepan. Pour in the bacon and spinach and stir to mix. Serve immediately with the grated cheese.

Creamy Pasta with Sun-dried Tomatoes, Olives and Pine Nuts

SERVES 4-6 / VEGETARIAN

I like to use semi-sun-dried tomatoes for this simple dish, as they are milder and more juicy than the completely sun-dried ones. Leave out the olives if your children don't care for them.

14 oz dried pasta
1 c crème fraîche
3 oz sun-dried tomatoes
1 tbsp tomato paste
12–16 black olives, pitted and chopped
2 oz pine nuts, toasted in a dry pan until golden
2 oz Parmesan cheese, finely grated
Salt and freshly ground black pepper
Pinch of sugar (optional)

Bring a large saucepan of water with 1 teaspoon salt up to the boil, and cook the pasta according to the instructions on the packet.

Meanwhile, place the crème fraîche in a saucepan and heat to a gentle simmer. Add the sun-dried tomatoes, tomato paste, chopped olives, most of the toasted pine nuts and most of the grated cheese. Season with salt and pepper and taste—it might need a pinch of sugar too.

When the pasta is cooked, drain, leaving a couple of tablespoons of the cooking water with the pasta. Stir in the hot sun-dried tomato sauce, taste and season again if necessary. Sprinkle with the remaining pine nuts and grated Parmesan cheese and serve.

RACHEL'S HANDY TIP
Try drizzling Basil Pesto (see page 217) over this dish. It's also good with slices of chorizo sausage that have been cooked in a hot dry pan for a minute.

Spicy Salmon Cakes

SERVES 4-6

This foolproof recipe makes about 12 salmon cakes for a family supper. You can also use this recipe to make about 40 mini salmon cakes for small bites to serve with drinks for an informal party. They are absolutely delicious served with flavored mayonnaise (see page 216) and Tomato and Cucumber Salsa (see page 139). Again, if your children do not eat spicy food, you can omit the chile or Tabasco.

3/4 lb filleted and skinned salmon, roughly chopped
4 tbsp (1/2 stick) butter
2-3 garlic cloves, peeled and crushed
4 oz fresh white breadcrumbs
1 egg, whisked
2 tsp Dijon mustard
2 tbsp lemon juice
2 tbsp chopped fresh cilantro (you can chop the small stalks too)
6 scallions, chopped
2 tsp Worcestershire sauce
1-2 tsp Tabasco sauce or 1 deseeded and chopped chile (optional for children)
3-4 tbsp olive oil, for cooking

Combine all the ingredients except the olive oil in a food processor and whiz to combine. Taste for seasoning and add salt, pepper, and more lemon juice or Tabasco, if necessary. If you do not have a food processor, chop up the salmon as finely as possible and mix together all the ingredients in a bowl. Shape into 3-inch patties or 1 1/2-inch diameter patties for mini salmon cakes. Pan-fry in 3-4 tablespoons olive oil on a medium heat for 3-4 minutes on each side (2-3 minutes for mini cakes), or until golden. Serve on warm plates.

VARIATION
This is also delicious with a Mediterranean twist. Omit the Tabasco or chile and substitute the same amount of basil for the cilantro in the salmon cakes and serve with the mayonnaise and salsa.

Pan-fried Mackerel with Herb Butter

SERVES 4 AS A MAIN COURSE OR 8 AS A STARTER

Mackerel is a delicious and healthy fish. It is also serious brain food for children and adults alike. Mackerel is in season from late spring through the summer into September.

FOR THE HERB BUTTER:
8 tbsp (1 stick) butter, softened
2 tbsp chopped fresh herbs, such as dill or thyme
1 tbsp lemon juice
FOR THE MACKEREL:
8 fillets of mackerel, with the skins on
3/4 c (3 oz) all-purpose flour, seasoned with salt and pepper
2 tbsp butter, softened
Lemon wedges, to serve

First, make the herb butter. Cream the butter in a bowl, add the chopped herbs and the lemon juice. Roll into a sausage shape and wrap in wax paper or plastic wrap. Put into the freezer to chill quickly.

Place a frying pan or a grill pan on the heat and wait for it to get very hot. When the pan is hot, dip the fillets of fish in the seasoned flour and shake off the excess. Spread the flesh side (not the skin side) with a little soft butter and place butter-side-down on the hot pan. Cook for a couple of minutes, until crisp and golden, then turn over and cook the other side for another 2–3 minutes, turning down the heat if the pan is getting too hot. Serve on hot plates with one or two slices of herb butter slowly melting on the fish, and a wedge of lemon on the side.

Upside-down Rhubarb and Ginger Cake

SERVES 8 / VEGETARIAN

This recipe and the variation opposite are great topsy-turvy desserts and they are wonderfully easy because they are made in a frying pan instead of a cake pan. When I made this for one of my television programs, the film crew declared it to be the best thing ever!

4 tbsp (1/2 stick) butter
1 c plus 2 tbsp (9 oz) light brown sugar
12 oz rhubarb, trimmed and cut into
　3/4-in chunks
1 2/3 c (7 oz) all-purpose flour
1 tsp baking powder
1/2 tsp salt

1/4 tsp baking soda
2 eggs
3/4 c plus 2 tbsp buttermilk or
　sour milk
1/3 c vegetable or sunflower oil
1 generous tsp of grated ginger

Preheat the oven to 350°F (180°C). Melt the butter in a medium-sized (10-inch) ovenproof frying pan. Stir in half the sugar and cook over a gentle heat for about 2 minutes. Add the rhubarb—there's no need to stir—and remove from the heat and set aside.

Sift the flour, baking powder, salt and baking soda into a bowl. Whisk the eggs in a measuring cup or small bowl and add the remaining sugar, buttermilk, oil and ginger. Mix together, then pour into the dry ingredients and whisk to form a liquid batter. Pour this over the rhubarb in the pan. Place the pan in the oven and bake for 30 minutes or until the cake feels firm in the center.

Cool for 5 minutes before turning out by placing an inverted plate over the top of the pan and turning pan and plate over together in one quick movement. Serve warm or at room temperature with softly whipped cream.

Upside-down Apple and Cinnamon Cake

SERVES 8 / VEGETARIAN

This variation on the upside-down theme is a perfect end to a special family meal or dinner party. If you have any left over (I certainly never do!), have it with a cup of tea the next day.

4 tbsp (1/2 stick) butter
1 c plus 2 tbsp light brown sugar
3 eating apples, peeled, cored
 and sliced 1/4 in thick
1 2/3 c (7 oz) all-purpose flour
1 tsp baking powder
1/2 tsp salt

1/4 tsp baking soda
1 generous tsp ground cinnamon
2 eggs
3/4 c plus 2 tbsp buttermilk or sour milk
1/3 c vegetable or sunflower oil
Whipped cream, to serve

Preheat the oven to 350°F (180°C). Melt the butter in a medium-sized (10-inch) ovenproof frying pan. Stir in half the sugar and cook over a gentle heat for about 2 minutes. Add the apple—there's no need to stir—and remove from the heat and set aside.

Sift the flour, baking powder, salt, baking soda and ground cinnamon into a bowl. Whisk the eggs in a measuring cup or small bowl and add the remaining sugar, buttermilk and oil. Mix together, then pour into the dry ingredients and whisk to combine into a liquid batter. Pour this over the apple in the pan. Place the pan in the preheated oven and bake for 30 minutes or until the cake feels firm in the center.

Cool for 5 minutes before turning out by placing an inverted plate over the top of the pan and turning pan and plate over together in one quick movement. Serve warm or at room temperature with softly whipped cream.

Toffee Sundae

MAKES 2¼ CUPS SAUCE / VEGETARIAN

My boys and I all love making sundaes. They're a serious treat! The toffee sauce is the best ever, and keeps for months in the fridge. It's especially delicious for drizzling over ice cream. This recipe makes quite a lot, but since it keeps for so long it's great to have some just waiting for an excuse to be used up.

FOR THE TOFFEE SAUCE:
8 tbsp (1 stick) butter
3/4 c (6 oz) light brown sugar
1/2 c (4 oz) superfine sugar
1 1/4 c corn syrup
1 c light cream
1/2 tsp vanilla extract

FOR THE SUNDAE:
1 tub vanilla ice cream
TO SERVE:
Pieces of Heavenly Fudge
    (see page 190) (optional)

For the toffee sauce, put all the ingredients into a saucepan, and boil for about 4–5 minutes, until the sauce is smooth, stirring regularly.

Place a scoop or two of vanilla ice cream in each bowl or glass. Drizzle over the warm toffee sauce and, if you like, crumble two or three pieces of Heavenly Fudge over each bowl and eat!

No-pastry Pear and Almond Tart

SERVES 6 / VEGETARIAN

This is a delicious tart and is also perfect for people who don't want to make pastry. You can use a variety of fruit for the filling (see below).

3/4 c (6 oz) confectioners' sugar
1/2 c (2 oz) all-purpose flour
4 oz almond meal
Finely grated zest of 1 lemon
5 egg whites
12 tbsp (1 1/2 sticks) butter, melted

2 ripe pears, peeled, cored and
  quartered, then cut into long slices
  about 1/4 in thick
2 tbsp slivered almonds
Confectioners' sugar, to serve

Preheat the oven to 400°F (200°C). Lightly grease the sides of a 9-inch tart pan with a removable bottom and place a disc of wax paper on the base. If you prefer, you can serve this tart on the tart pan base, in which case do not use the wax paper.

Sift the confectioners' sugar and flour into a bowl and stir in the almond meal and lemon zest. Whisk the egg whites for 30 seconds, until just frothy, and add to the dry ingredients with the warm melted butter. Mix until smooth.

Pour the mixture into the prepared pan. Arrange the pieces of pear on top and sprinkle with the slivered almonds.

Bake in the oven for 15 minutes, then turn down the oven to 350°F (180°C) and cook for a further 10 minutes or until risen and pale golden. The filling should feel firm to the touch in the center.

Allow to sit in the pan for a few minutes before turning out onto a wire rack. Dust with confectioners' sugar to serve. This is delicious with softly whipped cream.

VARIATIONS

Instead of pears I sometimes use 4 oz raspberries or blackberries (either fresh or frozen) for the topping. Alternatively, I use 2 oz pine nuts instead of fruit. You can also make this with 4 oz peach or nectarine slices, which is particularly nice in the summer!

2 Sweet Celebrations

I adore baking, and love having the excuse to make something sweet. It could be a birthday, anniversary, any other special occasion, or even just for a gossip and a cup of tea with a friend! People always reckon that you are a genius with lots of time on your hands if you have baked something, but really it's often only a matter of getting the oven on, and mixing together a few magic ingredients in a bowl. And what a gorgeous gift it is to make a homemade treat to celebrate someone's special day!

Cardamom Sour-Cream Cake

SERVES 6-8 / VEGETARIAN

This is one of the most delicious cakes. It stays wonderfully moist and the flavor of the sour cream or crème fraîche with the cardamom is sublime. This makes a gorgeous birthday cake, or a special gift for Mother's Day.

FOR THE CAKE:
1 egg
8-oz tub sour cream or crème fraîche
    (reserve 1 tbsp for icing)
3/4 c (6 oz) superfine sugar
13/4 c (8 oz) all-purpose flour, sifted

1/2 tsp baking soda
Pinch of salt
1 tsp ground cardamom seeds
FOR THE ICING:
1/2 c (4 oz) confectioners' sugar, sifted
1 tbsp sour cream or crème fraîche

Preheat the oven to 350°F (180°C). Grease the sides of an 8-inch round cake pan and dust with flour; line the base of the pan with a disc of wax paper.

Whisk the egg in a large bowl. Add all but 1 generous tablespoon of the sour cream or crème fraîche and the sugar and whisk to combine. Add the sifted flour and baking soda, then the salt and the ground cardamom. Fold the mixture to combine; do not overmix. Transfer into the pan and place in the oven. Cook for about 35 minutes, until the top of the cake just feels firm to the touch and a skewer inserted into the center comes out clean. Remove from the oven and let it sit for 10 minutes before removing from the pan and cooling on a wire rack.

When the cake has just cooled, make the icing by mixing the reserved tablespoon of sour cream or crème fraîche with the confectioners' sugar. If it is too stiff add just a drop of water; if it is too runny, add a bit more sugar. Spread the icing over the top of the cake, allowing any extra icing to drip down the sides.

VARIATION

CARDAMOM SOUR-CREAM CUPCAKES

This recipe works perfectly when cooked in a muffin pan. The cakes look so sweet with birthday candles in each one. Just divide the mixture between 12 muffin cups (use paper liners) and cook at the same temperature for 18-20 minutes. Ice as above.

Chocolate Cake for Birthday Parties

SERVES 8 / VEGETARIAN

I often make this for my children's birthday parties. One year my youngest requested a cake in the shape of a boy (well, Bob the Builder actually), and I did not have the cake pan required. So, I multiplied this recipe by three and cooked it in two roasting pans (each measuring 12 x 10 inches). When the cake was cooked, it took every bit of artistic talent that I had to cut it into something that slightly resembled our friend Bob. At least the guests at the party were only three years old, and had great imaginations!

FOR THE CAKE:
8 tbsp (1 stick) butter, softened
1$\frac{1}{2}$ c (12 oz) superfine sugar
2 eggs
1$\frac{3}{4}$ c (8 oz) all-purpose flour
$\frac{1}{2}$ c (2 oz) cocoa powder
1 tsp baking powder
$\frac{1}{4}$ tsp baking soda

1 c buttermilk or sour milk
1 tsp vanilla extract
FOR THE ICING:
1$\frac{1}{4}$ c (10 oz) confectioners' sugar
2 tsp cocoa powder
1 tbsp butter, melted
A few tbsp boiling water

Preheat the oven to 350°F (180°C). Line the bases of two 8-inch or three 7-inch cake pans with wax paper, and grease the sides.

Put the softened butter into a large bowl, add the sugar and beat together until light and fluffy; add the eggs one at a time, beating well. Sift the flour, cocoa, baking powder and baking soda into the butter and sugar mixture, then pour in the buttermilk and add the vanilla, stirring well to create a smooth cake dough.

Divide between the cake pans and place in the center of the preheated oven. Bake for 19–25 minutes, until just set in the center. When cooked, a skewer inserted into the center should come out clean. Allow to sit in the pans for 5 minutes, then turn out and cool on a wire rack.

Meanwhile, make the icing. Sift the confectioners' sugar and cocoa powder into a bowl, then beat in the butter and enough boiling (or hot) water to bring it to spreading consistency. It may take only 1 or 2 tablespoons of water.

Sandwich the cakes together with a layer of icing in the middle. To coat the cake in icing, I find it easiest to place it on an upturned plate. Use a small palette knife or a table knife, and dip it into hot water before and during the icing of the cake; I find this helps give a smooth icing with a shiny gloss.

Porter Cake

SERVES 10-12 / VEGETARIAN

This traditional Irish cake uses porter, such as Guinness, Beamish or Murphy's, and is a deliciously rich and moist fruit cake. Make it a few days in advance of the celebratory event (it's perfect for St. Patrick's Day) if you like, and it will improve even more!

$3^2/_3$ c (1 lb) all-purpose flour
1 tsp grated or ground nutmeg
1 tsp pumpkin pie spice
1 tsp baking powder
Pinch of salt
16 tbsp (2 sticks) butter, softened
1 c (8 oz) light brown sugar
1 lb golden or regular raisins or a mixture of both
3 oz chopped candied peel
2 eggs
One 12-oz bottle of porter or stout

Preheat the oven to 350°F (180°C). Line the sides and base of an 8-inch high-sided round cake pan (the sides should be about 23/4 inches high) with wax paper.

Sift the flour, nutmeg, pie spice, baking powder and salt into a bowl. Rub in the butter, then stir in the sugar, raisins and the candied peel.

Whisk the eggs in another bowl, add the porter or stout, then pour into the dry ingredients and mix well. Pour into the prepared pan and bake for about 2 hours in the preheated oven. If it starts to brown too quickly on top, cover it with foil or wax paper after about 1 hour. The cake is cooked when a skewer inserted into the center comes out clean. Allow it to sit in the pan for about 20 minutes before turning out and cooling on a wire rack.

Orange and Chocolate Chip Celebratory Cupcakes

MAKES 12 / VEGETARIAN

I love the combination of orange and choc chip, but if you just want plain cupcakes omit the zest and replace the juice with an equal quantity of milk. These would be great for a birthday breakfast!

FOR THE CUPCAKES:

2 eggs

1/2 c plus 2 tbsp (5 oz) light brown sugar

Finely grated zest and juice of
   two oranges

Milk

8 tbsp (1 stick) butter, melted

2 3/4 c (12 oz) all-purpose flour, sifted

1 tbsp baking powder

1/4 tsp baking soda

1/2 tsp salt

7 oz dark chocolate, roughly chopped
   into chips

FOR THE ICING:

1/2 c (4 oz) confectioners' sugar

Juice of 1/2 orange

Preheat the oven to 400°F (200°C). Line a muffin pan with 12 paper muffin liners.

Whisk the eggs and add the sugar and grated orange zest. Measure the juice from the oranges and add milk to make 3/4 cup. Whisk the juice, milk and melted butter into the eggs and sugar, then add the sifted flour, baking powder, baking soda, salt and the chopped chocolate. Stir to combine but do not overmix. Spoon the mixture into the muffin cups and bake in the oven for 18–25 minutes until golden on top and the center is firm to the touch.

When the cupcakes have cooled, make the orange icing. Sift the confectioners' sugar into a bowl and add 1 teaspoon orange juice. Stir and add a little more juice. Beat the mixture until it comes together and add yet another drop of juice to make an icing of spreadable consistency. If you have made it too wet, add a little more sifted confectioners' sugar.

When the icing is made and the cupcakes are cool, take a small table knife and dip it into a cup of boiling water. This will make it easier to spread the icing on the cupcakes and give it a nice glossy shine. Spread the icing (about 1 teaspoon per cupcake) onto each cake, allow the icing to set for a few minutes and then serve. These cakes keep very well for 4–5 days and can also be frozen.

Lemon Cookies
MAKES ABOUT 25 / VEGETARIAN

These are incredibly simple and gorgeous cookies. Do make sure that the butter you use is nice and soft. They are very tasty on their own with a cup of tea or with the Lemon and Ginger Pudding (see page 171). The cookies can be cut into any kind of shape, such as hearts for Valentine's Day, numbers for a birthday party or little holly leaves or Christmas trees during the festive season.

1½ c (6 oz) all-purpose flour
Finely grated zest of 1 lemon
8 tbsp (1 stick) butter, softened
¼ c (2 oz) superfine sugar

Preheat the oven to 350°F (180°C). Put the flour and lemon zest into a mixing bowl, rub in the soft butter, add the sugar and bring the whole mixture together to form a stiff dough. Do not add any water.

Roll the dough out to a thickness of about ¼ inch and cut into shapes. Transfer carefully to a baking sheet and bake in the oven for 6–10 minutes until they are pale golden. Cool on a wire rack.

RACHEL'S HANDY TIP
I quite often roll out this dough between two sheets of plastic wrap, as I do for pastry. Chill the slightly flattened piece of dough before rolling out and then the butter does not stick to the plastic.

Whole Wheat Shortbread Cookies

MAKES ABOUT 20 / VEGETARIAN

My boys love making these cookies so they can choose whatever shapes they like. They are great for birthday parties and lunch boxes. They are also good sandwiched together with raspberry jam!

3/4 c (3 oz) whole wheat flour
3/4 c (3 oz) all-purpose flour
8 tbsp (1 stick) butter, softened
1/4 c (2 oz) superfine sugar

Preheat the oven to 350°F (180°C). Place all the ingredients in a food processor and whiz until the mixture almost comes together and resembles coarse breadcrumbs. Then tip onto the work surface and bring it together with your hands. If you are not using a food processor, rub the butter into the combined flour and sugar in a bowl and bring together with your hands.

Sprinkle your work surface with a little flour (wheat or white) and roll out the dough until it is about 1/4 inch thick (or roll it between two pieces of plastic wrap, as in the note on page 45). Using a cookie cutter, cut into whatever shapes you like or just simply into squares with a knife. Transfer onto a baking sheet (no need to grease or line it) and bake in the oven for 6–10 minutes depending on the size, or until the cookies are pale golden and feel firm on top. Remove carefully and cool on a wire rack.

Little Almond Brittles

MAKES ABOUT 40 / VEGETARIAN

These are divine little petits-fours, great to serve at the end of a special celebratory meal with coffee. They also make a lovely gift when placed in a small see-through bag and tied with a ribbon.

4 oz slivered almonds
1 c (8 oz) superfine sugar
6 tbsp water
6 tbsp (3/4 stick) butter
4 oz good-quality dark chocolate with at least 70% cocoa solids, chopped

Preheat the oven to 350°F (180°C). Line two baking sheets with wax paper or parchment.

Place the almonds on a baking sheet and toast in the oven for 3–4 minutes until golden—watch them carefully to ensure they don't burn.

Place the sugar, water and butter in a saucepan and stir over a low heat until the sugar has dissolved and the butter melted. Stop stirring, bring to the boil, and boil uncovered for 10–15 minutes or until the mixture is golden brown— watch out as it will be very hot. Do not overstir this; just swirl the mixture in the pan to prevent it from burning on the bottom. Remove from the heat and add the almonds. Stir to combine; do not overstir or the mix will turn sugary. Working quickly, place heaping teaspoons of the mixture on the lined baking sheets and flatten with the back of a wet spoon. Return the pan to the heat for a few seconds if it gets too thick.

Melt the chocolate in a bowl over a pan of simmering water, and drizzle over the brittles (or if you prefer, you can dip the tops of the brittles in the melted chocolate). Allow the chocolate to set, then remove them from the baking sheet and serve or wrap up for gifts. They will keep for a couple of weeks in an airtight container.

Chocolate and Almond Cake with Brandy Cream

SERVES 8 / VEGETARIAN

This is a delicious chocolate cake that uses ground almonds instead of flour, which makes it wonderfully moist. It's an excellent grown-up birthday cake, but if you wish to make this for children, fill it with whipped cream and raspberries instead.

FOR THE CAKE:
4 1/2 oz dark chocolate, chopped
4 eggs
2/3 c (5 oz) superfine sugar
5 oz ground almonds
Confectioners' sugar, for dusting
FOR THE BRANDY CREAM:
6 tbsp heavy cream
1-2 tbsp confectioners' sugar
2 tbsp brandy (or another liqueur like rum or Cointreau)

Preheat the oven to 350°F (180°C). Prepare two 8-inch cake pans by oiling the sides and lining the bases with discs of wax paper. Melt the chocolate in a bowl by setting it over a saucepan of gently simmering water.

While the chocolate is melting, place the eggs and sugar in a stand mixer and whisk for about 5-8 minutes until light and frothy. When the chocolate has melted, allow to cool for a minute, then pour the egg and sugar mixture gradually onto the chocolate, stirring all the time, and mix until combined. Gently stir in the ground almonds.

Divide the mixture between the two prepared pans and place in the preheated oven. Cook for 17-22 minutes (in my oven they usually take 19 minutes) until the tops of the cakes feel firm in the center. Allow to cool in the pans for about 10 minutes before carefully transferring to a cooling rack. As they cool, the tops and sides of the cakes will crisp up and crack a little.

Meanwhile, make the brandy cream. Whip the cream until just stiff and fold in the sifted confectioners' sugar and brandy. Spread the brandy cream on one cake. Sandwich the cakes together and dust with confectioners' sugar.

Sponge Cake with Rhubarb Cream

SERVES 6-8 / VEGETARIAN

This is a classic sponge cake, made all the more gorgeous with the rhubarb cream filling. Also try filling it with raspberry jam and whipped cream, sliced strawberries and whipped cream, or with fresh, hand-picked blackberries and cream. This is perfect for Father's or Mother's Day (that's a hint, boys!) or, of course, as a birthday cake.

FOR THE CAKE:
9 tbsp butter, softened
3/4 c (6 oz) superfine sugar
3 eggs
1 1/2 c (6 oz) all-purpose flour
1 tsp baking powder
1 tbsp milk
Confectioners' sugar or superfine
   sugar, for dusting

FOR THE RHUBARB CREAM:
4 oz rhubarb, trimmed and sliced
1/4 c (2 oz) sugar
1/4 c water
1/3 c heavy cream

Preheat the oven to 350°F (180°C). Grease and flour the sides of two 8-inch cake pans, and line the bases with discs of wax paper.

Cream the butter until soft, then gradually add the sugar, and beat until light and fluffy. Add the eggs one by one, beating well all the time. Sift the flour and baking powder, and stir in gently, then stir in the milk until just combined.

Divide the mixture between the two pans, hollowing it slightly in the center, so that it will be flat on top when cooked. Bake for 20-25 minutes, or until the center of the cake springs back when you push it gently. Turn out onto a wire rack and allow it to cool. (Place the cake that will become the top layer on its base so that the top isn't marked by the cooling rack.)

Meanwhile, place the sliced rhubarb, sugar and water in a saucepan, cover and cook over a gentle heat for about 10 minutes, until the rhubarb is soft. Take off the lid and boil while stirring until it is thick. Pour into a bowl and allow to cool. Whip the cream until it forms soft peaks, then fold in the rhubarb. Sandwich the cakes with the rhubarb cream and sprinkle with sifted confectioners' or superfine sugar.

3 Picnics and Days Out

Why is it that food eaten outside just tastes so much better? Even a simple sandwich and a cup of tea tastes like the best meal you have ever had! But something you've made yourself is bound to be a lot more delicious than anything you might buy. I love preparing food to take on a picnic or to the beach, or to bring to the woods for a mid-walk snack (a good incentive to get the children out walking). You might only go as far as your own back garden, it doesn't matter. My children love the novelty of gathering up the picnic blanket, putting food in a basket and finding a nice spot to eat. I'm sure the fresh air makes them eat that bit more too, which is always good!

Muffleta

SERVES 6-8

This is made from a hollowed-out loaf of bread with the top cut off and saved to make the lid. It's filled with layers of different fillings, then pressed for a few hours and cut into wedges so that each slice has a bit of crust surrounding a wonderful layered filling. It looks so impressive, but could not be easier to make. Vary the ingredients according to your taste. It's best if made a day in advance, so it can be pressed overnight in the fridge.

4 red onions, peeled and cut into
   wedges
1 tbsp olive oil
Sea salt and freshly ground pepper
1 round loaf of bread about 8 inches
   in diameter
2 tbsp Basil Pesto (see page 217), mixed
   with 1 tbsp olive oil
3 slices Parma or Serrano ham,
   optional

4 Preserved Roasted Peppers (see
   page 177)
8 oz soft goat cheese, cut into slices
1 tbsp Olive Paste (see page 102),
   mixed with 1 tbsp olive oil
6-8 thin slices of salami, optional
1 large handful of arugula leaves

Preheat the oven to 400°F (200°C). Toss the red onion with the olive oil on a baking sheet, season and roast in the oven for 10–15 minutes or until soft. Set aside.

Using a serrated bread knife, slice the top off the loaf of bread and set aside until later. Scoop out most of the bread from inside the loaf and put to one side.

Spread the pesto and olive oil around the inside of the loaf and the cut side of the lid. Place half the Parma or Serrano ham in the base of the loaf, if using, then half of the pieces of roast peppers, followed by half the goat cheese. Then drizzle half the olive paste over the cheese, followed by the slices of salami, if using, and then the roasted red onions and last the arugula.

Season with sea salt and pepper and repeat with the second half of all the ingredients. You might need to press it down gently with the palms of your hands to fit everything in—it should be very full or it will fall apart when you try to slice it. When you have finished with all the ingredients, place the lid on top.

Wrap the loaf in plastic, put it on a plate, then place a side plate or board with weights or even jars of jam or anything heavy on top and place in the fridge. This will weigh it down, which will make it easier to cut into slices. Leave for 3 hours to 1 day, unwrap and cut into wedges to serve.

RACHEL'S HANDY TIP
You can always whiz up the discarded bread to make breadcrumbs for the freezer.

Chest of Sandwiches

MAKES ABOUT 15 SANDWICHES

This was ingeniously created by my husband's grandmother, Myrtle Allen. It's similar to the muffleta on the previous page, but for this you open the top of a loaf of bread like a flap, cut out the inside, make little sandwiches out of what you've taken out and miraculously pop them all back into the hollow "chest." What could be better to take on a long walk or to the races? Talk about picnic envy!

2-lb rectangular loaf of unsliced bread
Sandwich fillings, such as Cheddar cheese and chutney (see pages 178–81);
 cooked chicken mixed with Mayonnaise (see page 216); smoked salmon
 and Cucumber Pickle (see page 174)

Insert a bread knife into one long side of the loaf, just above the bottom crust. Push the knife through until it reaches, but does not go through, the crust on the far side. Without making the cut through which the knife was inserted any bigger, work the knife in a fan shape from side to side, then pull it out. The bread should now be cut away from the bottom crust inside but without a very noticeable mark on the exterior of the loaf. This takes some practice, so you may wish to have an extra loaf the first time.

Next, cut through the top of the loaf to make a lid, carefully leaving one long side uncut as a hinge. When you open it, if it looks in danger of falling off, keep it propped up from behind with a couple of jars or something similar.

Finally, with the lid open, cut the bread away from the sides just inside of the crust on all sides and down to 1/2 inch of the bottom crust. Ease the bread out carefully—it should turn out in a solid brick, leaving an empty case behind.

Cut the brick into four long, horizontal slices (cut it in half lengthwise first to make it easier if you like) and make two long sandwiches using the fillings of your choice. Cut each big sandwich into four or five small finger sandwiches, press them together firmly and put them back into the chest. Surprise your friends by presenting the loaf and letting them open it up to find the treasure inside!

Salad of White Beans with Tomatoes and Tuna
SERVES 3-4 / VEGETARIAN

This is one of those great salads that can be put together in no time. It's fresh and delicious and is made from ingredients that you're likely to have in your kitchen at any time.

FOR THE DRESSING:
3 tbsp olive oil
2 tbsp lemon juice
Salt and freshly ground black pepper

FOR THE SALAD:
One 15-oz can navy or cannellini beans, drained

One 7-oz can tuna, drained and broken into chunks
5 oz cherry tomatoes, quartered
2 scallions, trimmed and thinly sliced
1-2 tbsp chopped fresh marjoram or mint

In a small bowl, mix together the olive oil, lemon juice and seasoning. Assemble the remaining ingredients in a bowl and then drizzle with the dressing and toss.

Arugula, Tomato and Sugar Snap Pea Salad
SERVES 4-6 / VEGETARIAN

This is also a lovely fresh, light summer salad.

FOR THE DRESSING:
2 tbsp olive oil
1 tbsp lemon juice or cider vinegar
1/2 tsp whole-grain mustard
Pinch of sugar
Salt and freshly ground black pepper

FOR THE SALAD:
6 oz sugar snap peas, trimmed
5 oz arugula
9 oz cherry tomatoes, halved or quartered

Whisk the dressing ingredients together and season to taste. Bring a pan of salted water up to the boil and add the peas. Boil for 2-3 minutes, until they still have a bit of bite, then drain and refresh in cold water and pat dry. Mix the peas, arugula and cherry tomatoes in a bowl. Drizzle the dressing over the salad and toss.

Duck, Lentil and Red Cabbage Salad

SERVES 4-6

This is a really delicious and very portable salad, and can also be prepared in advance. Leftover roast chicken works well as a substitute for the duck breast.

½ lb duck breast
Salt and freshly ground black pepper
2 oz hazelnuts
½ lb lentils
¼ c olive oil
Juice of 1 lemon
½-1 red chile, deseeded and finely chopped
¼ red cabbage, about 11 oz, core removed and very thinly sliced
3 tbsp chopped fresh cilantro

Preheat the oven to 400°F (200°C). Using the tip of a knife, make three or four shallow incisions through the skin of the duck breast. Season the fat side with salt and pepper and drizzle with a tiny bit of olive oil. Place fat-side-down in an unheated frying pan or grill pan. Turn the heat on low and cook the duck breast very slowly, until golden brown, allowing the fat to render out—this may take 15-20 minutes. Turn the duck breast over and continue to cook for another 5-10 minutes, until it is just cooked through, or pop it into the oven on a roasting pan for the final 5-10 minutes.

Meanwhile, roast the hazelnuts by tossing them in a dry frying pan over a medium heat until golden, or put them into the oven with the duck for 5-7 minutes—but on a separate roasting pan. Chop roughly when cool enough to handle.

While the duck is cooking, put the lentils in a saucepan and cover with cold water, bring up to the boil and cook for 15-20 minutes until soft. Drain and toss with the olive oil, lemon juice and chopped chile and season to taste. Add the sliced red cabbage and chopped cilantro and stir to mix. Taste and add a little more olive oil if it is a bit dry or more lemon juice if it needs sharpening up.

When the duck is cooked and has cooled slightly, slice it very thinly and toss with the salad. Tip into a large bowl or pile onto salad plates and sprinkle with the chopped roasted hazelnuts.

Asparagus and Scallion Tart

SERVES 6-8 / VEGETARIAN

This is one of the very best savory tarts and it is perfect in the late spring/early summer when asparagus is in season. It is light and delicate in flavor, and has a wonderful crisp shortcrust pastry base.

10-in Shortcrust Pastry shell, baked blind (see page 220)
1 tbsp olive oil
7 oz scallions, trimmed and finely sliced or chopped
7 oz asparagus spears, trimmed
Salt and freshly ground black pepper
4 eggs
1½ c heavy cream
1 oz Parmesan cheese, finely grated

Preheat the oven to 350°F (180°C). To make the tart filling, heat the olive oil in a small saucepan, add the scallions and cook over a low heat until soft. Cook the asparagus by dropping it into boiling water with a pinch of salt, cover and bring back up to the boil, then remove the lid and boil, uncovered, for 3-4 minutes until it is just cooked. Drain, and then slice the asparagus into 1½-inch pieces, at an angle.

Whisk the eggs in a bowl, add the cream and the cooked scallions and season. Pour this filling into the cooked pastry shell, still in the pan. Drop the asparagus into the tart and sprinkle the grated Parmesan cheese over the top. Carefully place the tart into the preheated oven and cook for 20-30 minutes, or until the tart is just set in the center. Remove from the oven, and serve out of the pan, hot or at room temperature.

Potato, Chorizo and Feta Frittata
SERVES 8

A frittata is the best thing to eat outdoors and is just as fantastic hot or cold. For a vegetarian option you can leave out the chorizo.

9 oz potatoes, peeled and cut
  into ½-in cubes
6 tbsp olive oil
1 onion, peeled and sliced
8 eggs
6 tbsp light cream

1 tsp salt
1 tbsp chopped fresh marjoram
4 oz chorizo, sliced
4 oz feta cheese, crumbled

Preheat the oven to 350°F (180°C). Place the potatoes in a saucepan, cover with boiling water and boil for 5 minutes, or until just cooked. Do not overcook or they will go mushy. Drain and set aside.

Heat a 10-inch ovenproof frying pan, add 3 tablespoons of olive oil and the sliced onion, cover with a saucepan lid and sweat over a gentle heat until soft and slightly golden. Set aside.

Whisk the eggs in a bowl, add the cream, the salt and the marjoram. Stir in the sliced chorizo, the cooked onion and potatoes.

Heat 3 tablespoons of olive oil in the frying pan. When it is hot, pour in the egg mixture and stir briefly to distribute the ingredients evenly. Top with the crumbled feta cheese. Place in the preheated oven and bake for 25-35 minutes or until set in the center. Remove from the oven and allow to cool a little before sliding it onto a large serving plate or a large cake pan lined with baking parchment, if you want to transport it on a picnic. Serve warm or at room temperature.

VARIATION

BUTTERNUT SQUASH, CHORIZO AND FETA FRITTATA

Follow the recipe above but replace the potato with the same weight of butternut squash, peeled (with a knife), deseeded and cubed.

Ham and Egg Pie
SERVES 6-8

This is such a lovely, old-fashioned picnic pie.

**7 oz Shortcrust Pastry, made with 1 c plus 2 tbsp (4$\frac{1}{2}$ oz) flour,
6 tbsp ($\frac{3}{4}$ stick) butter, pinch of salt and $\frac{1}{2}$-1 egg, following
the instructions on page 220**

FOR THE FILLING:

1 tbsp butter
1 onion, peeled and chopped
6 eggs
$\frac{1}{3}$ c heavy cream
5 oz cooked ham or bacon, sliced into $\frac{1}{2}$ x $\frac{3}{4}$-in pieces
1 tbsp chopped parsley
Salt and freshly ground black pepper

Preheat the oven to 350°F (180°C). Roll out the pastry and line a 10-inch ovenproof pie plate with it. Trim the pastry so that it is a bit bigger than the plate, and then fold up the edges slightly so that you have a slight lip all the way around. This will prevent the cream from running over when you put it in the oven. Place the pastry in the fridge while you prepare the filling ingredients.

For the filling, melt the butter in a small saucepan, add the onion and cook over a gentle heat until soft. Whisk two of the eggs in a bowl, add the cream, the cooked onion, chopped ham and parsley. Season with salt and pepper to taste. Pour this into the pastry shell. Carefully break the remaining eggs onto the tart, trying to keep the egg yolks intact.

Bake for 25–35 minutes in the preheated oven until the custard is set in the center and the eggs on top are just cooked. Serve warm or allow to cool and pack for a picnic. Cut slices of the tart straight from the dish.

Maple Syrup and Pecan Muffins

MAKES 12 / VEGETARIAN

These are gorgeous muffins and are great for a picnic or children's lunch boxes.
They will keep for 4–5 days and also freeze well.

FOR THE MUFFINS:

1 egg

½ c (2 oz) rolled oats

⅓ c maple syrup

1 c milk

6 tbsp (¾ stick) butter, softened not melted

6 tbsp (3 oz) light brown sugar

1¾ c (8 oz) all-purpose flour, sifted

1 tbsp baking powder

½ tsp salt

3 oz chopped pecans or walnuts

FOR THE GLAZE (OPTIONAL):

4 tbsp (½ stick) butter, softened

¼ c (2 oz) confectioners' sugar, sifted

1 tbsp maple syrup

12 pecans

Preheat the oven to 400°F (200°C). Line a muffin pan with 12 paper muffin liners.

Whisk the egg in a bowl, add the oats, maple syrup and milk and whisk to combine. Set aside to soak while you prepare the other ingredients.

In a large bowl beat the butter, add the sugar, and mix to make a soft paste. Gradually add the milk mixture, stirring all the time, then stir in the sifted flour, baking powder, salt and chopped nuts, until just combined. Do not overstir.

Spoon the mixture into the muffin cups and bake in the preheated oven for 18–25 minutes until the tops are golden and feel firm to the touch in the center. Take out of the pan and allow to cool on a wire rack.

Make the glaze, if using, by mixing together the butter, sugar and syrup. Using a knife, spread the glaze over the tops of the cooled muffins and top each muffin with a pecan.

Jam Tarts

MAKES 12 / VEGETARIAN

These are a great way to use up leftover sweet or savory pastry; my children love making them for our picnics. There are few things more delicious on a picnic than a jam tart with a cup of tea, so don't forget to bring some in a thermos!

1/3 recipe (5 oz) Sweet or Savory Shortcrust Pastry (see page 220)
1/4 c apricot, raspberry or strawberry jam

Preheat the oven to 400°F (200°C). Roll out the pastry between two sheets of plastic wrap to a thickness of about 1/8 inch. Using a 2 1/2-inch cutter, cut out 12 rounds (you may need to gather up the scraps and reroll the pastry).

Press the rounds into a shallow tartlet pan (you can use paper liners if you wish) and drop a teaspoon of jam into each. Cook in the preheated oven for 8–12 minutes until the pastry is golden and the jam bubbling. Allow to cool slightly in the pan before carefully transferring to a wire rack (the jam will thicken as it cools).

4 Food for Children

People often ask me what I cook for my children and how I get them to eat good nutritious food. Well, in this chapter I have included many of my boys' favorite things to eat so that you can see for yourself there is no trick—it just tastes good! This is simple, foolproof, no-fuss food that is easy to prepare, which makes it ideal if your children want to help you in the kitchen. I have included great ideas for breakfast, lunch, supper and for yummy snacks as well.

Yogurt with Oats and Honey

SERVES 1 / VEGETARIAN

This is more a simple combination than a recipe, and is a fantastic, healthy, and very quick breakfast. The oats, with their slow-releasing carbohydrates, will keep your little ones going until lunch. Add some fruit too, if you wish, such as raspberries, blueberries, sliced strawberries, peaches or pears.

4–6 tbsp really good yogurt, plain or with fruit
1 small handful of rolled oats
1 tsp honey

Place the yogurt in a bowl, sprinkle with oats, drizzle with honey and serve.

Scrambled Eggs on Toast

SERVES 2 / VEGETARIAN

There is nothing like a classic scrambled egg on toast for breakfast or brunch, or even supper! Made in about two minutes, it's a perfect quick meal for hungry kids.

3 free-range eggs, best quality possible
2 tbsp milk (a little light cream mixed with the milk is, of course, divine!)
Salt and freshly ground black pepper
2 slices whole wheat bread
1 tbsp butter

Break the eggs into a bowl, add the milk and seasoning, and whisk for about 10 seconds. Pop the slices of bread in the toaster. Put the butter into a cold saucepan, add the egg mixture and stir continuously with a wooden spoon over a low heat until the mixture looks scrambled but still soft and creamy. Check the seasoning and serve, piled onto buttered toast.

Super Smoothies

EACH SERVES 4-6 / VEGETARIAN

Smoothies are a great way to get little ones to have some fruit, and my children love these combinations in particular. The Nectarine, Berry and Plum Smoothie has oats in it, which will keep children's energy topped up for a few hours as the oats contain slow-releasing carbohydrates. It's good for their concentration levels, too.

BANANA AND CINNAMON SMOOTHIE

4 bananas
2 ¼ c plain yogurt
2-4 tsp honey
1 tsp ground cinnamon

Whiz all the ingredients together in a blender or food processor and serve.

NECTARINE, BERRY AND PLUM SMOOTHIE

2 nectarines, stones removed
2 tbsp raspberries, blueberries or blackberries
2 plums, stones removed
13/4 c plain yogurt
2 tbsp rolled oats
Juice of ½ lemon
1 tbsp honey
10 ice cubes (optional)

Whiz all the ingredients together in a blender or food processor, adding more honey or lemon juice if you prefer a sweeter or sharper flavor respectively.

Quesadillas

MAKES 8 WEDGES / VEGETARIAN

Quesadillas are essentially the Central American toasted cheese sandwich! We make many versions of it at home, depending on what is in the fridge. Our children love plain cheese quesadillas or quesadillas filled with chicken or a little spinach (very handy as you can sneak it in almost unnoticed to greens-wary little ones). These are perfect for a snack or TV supper, and they are great for grown-ups too. I quite often have guacamole and tomato salsa with mine, as they do in Mexico, or else for a very fast sauce try Crème Fraîche with Sweet Chili (see page 139). Not all children like chile, but one of our boys actually likes it, so I sometimes leave it in for him.

2 wheat flour tortillas
4 oz cheese (I like a mixture of Cheddar,
    Gruyère and mozzarella), grated
1 scallion, trimmed and sliced (optional)
1/2 green or red chile, deseeded and chopped finely
    (optional—chiles can be very hot!)

Heat a frying pan slightly. Place one tortilla in the pan and sprinkle with all the grated cheese, the sliced scallion and chile, if using. Cover with the other tortilla and press down with a spatula or your hands. The cheese will have started melting at this stage and the tortilla on the bottom should be golden brown. When it is, carefully turn it over and then cook the other side for another couple of minutes, until it is golden and all the cheese has melted. Transfer to a board and cut into wedges. Serve immediately on its own or with Crème Fraîche with Sweet Chili or Tomato and Cucumber Salsa (see page 139).

VARIATIONS

QUESADILLAS WITH CHICKEN
Make as for the basic quesadillas, but add 3 oz shredded cooked chicken with the grated cheese.

QUESADILLAS WITH SPINACH
Make as for the basic quesadillas, but add one handful of baby spinach leaves (1/2 oz) with the grated cheese.

Parmesan Chicken Fingers

SERVES 6-8

These are one of my boys' favorite foods. Use good-quality free-range chicken and you'll have a delicious and nutritious meal that little ones will adore. My children love dipping these into homemade Tomato Ketchup (see page 80) or Mayonnaise (see page 216), or sometimes a mixture of the two!

1 lb 6 oz boneless and skinless chicken
½ c (2 oz) all-purpose flour
Salt and freshly ground black pepper
2 eggs, beaten
1 c (4 oz) fresh breadcrumbs

2 oz Parmesan cheese,
    or something similar, such as
    Grana Padano, finely grated
3 tbsp sunflower oil

These can be cooked on the stove top or in the oven. If using the oven, preheat to 400°F (200°C) and place a baking sheet in the oven to preheat.

Cut the chicken into strips the size of a big finger (½ x 4 inches). Place the flour in a mixing bowl or in a plastic bag with some salt and pepper. Place the beaten eggs in another bowl. Mix the breadcrumbs and finely grated cheese together and place in a bowl or bag as well.

Toss the chicken strips in the seasoned flour, making sure they do not stick together, then remove. Shake off the excess flour and dip them in the beaten egg. Remove from the egg, letting the excess drip off, and toss into the breadcrumb and cheese mix. Shake off the excess and lay the strips on a plate.

To cook on the stove, heat the oil in a large frying pan over a medium to high heat. When the oil is hot, add the chicken in a single layer; cook on one side for about 3 minutes until golden, then turn down the heat and flip the pieces over. Cook on the other side for about 4 minutes, until cooked through and golden.

To cook the chicken in the oven, drizzle the preheated baking sheet with the oil and lay the floured and seasoned strips in a single layer. Bake in the oven for about 12–18 minutes, turning them halfway through, or when golden on one side. When they are completely cooked, remove from the oven and serve.

PARMESAN FISH FINGERS

Prepare as for chicken, but substitute skinned and filleted fish. Cut into finger-size strips as before. For this recipe I use firm fish, such as cod or haddock. Cooking time remains the same.

Tomato Ketchup

MAKES 1 3/4 CUPS / VEGETARIAN

If your children regularly eat ketchup, then you might want to give them something a bit healthier and more delicious, like this real tomato ketchup. If you think they won't like this version, ease them into it by mixing some into their usual type and gradually adjust their taste. This is definitely best made in the summer with ripe red tomatoes.

2 tbsp olive oil
1/2 lb onions, peeled and
　roughly chopped
1 lb 6 oz tomatoes, roughly chopped
　(no need to peel)
2 garlic cloves, peeled and crushed
1/3 c white wine vinegar

6 tbsp (3 oz) sugar
2 tsp Dijon mustard
1/2 tsp ground allspice
1/2 tsp ground cloves
1/2 tsp salt
1/2 tsp freshly ground black pepper

Heat the olive oil in a saucepan, add the onions and toss over a medium heat until cooked and a little golden. Add the rest of the ingredients and simmer with the lid on for about 30 minutes, until very soft.

Remove from the heat and whiz in a blender or food processor. Pour through a sieve into a clean saucepan and simmer, uncovered and stirring regularly, for another 30 minutes, or until the mixture is thick.

Pour into sterilized jars or bottles (see page 177) and cover with lids.

Classic Spaghetti and Meatballs with Fresh Tomato Sauce

SERVES 6 (OR ABOUT 10 CHILDREN)

We used to have meatballs when we were little, and now our boys love them too. Children just love slurping up the spaghetti!

FOR THE MEATBALLS:
2 tbsp olive oil
1 onion, peeled and finely chopped
1 garlic clove, peeled and crushed
2 lb freshly ground beef
2 tbsp chopped fresh herbs, such as marjoram, or a smaller quantity of rosemary
1 egg, beaten
Salt and freshly ground black pepper

FOR THE TOMATO SAUCE:
3 tbsp olive oil
4 oz onion, peeled and sliced
1 garlic clove, peeled and crushed
Two 14½-oz cans chopped tomatoes, or 2 lb ripe, peeled (see page 178) and chopped tomatoes
Salt, freshly ground black pepper and sugar

TO SERVE:
3 tbsp olive oil
5 oz mozzarella, grated
1 lb spaghetti

To make the meatballs, heat the olive oil in a heavy, stainless-steel saucepan over a gentle heat and add the onion and garlic. Cover and sweat for 4 minutes, until soft and a little golden, then allow to cool.

In a bowl, mix the beef with the cold sweated onion and garlic, then add the herbs and the beaten egg. Season the mixture to taste. Fry a tiny bit to check the seasoning and adjust if necessary. Divide the mixture into about 24 round balls and place in a dish. Cover the meatballs and refrigerate until required.

Meanwhile, make the tomato sauce. Heat the oil in a stainless-steel saucepan. Add the sliced onion and crushed garlic, toss until coated, cover and sweat over a gentle heat until soft and a tiny bit golden. Add the tomatoes, mix and season with salt, freshly ground pepper and a pinch of sugar. Gently simmer, uncovered, for approximately 30 minutes or until softened.

Heat a frying pan over a medium heat with about 3 tablespoons of olive oil. Cook the meatballs for about 10 minutes. When they are done, transfer to a dish, add the tomato sauce and sprinkle the grated cheese on top. Place under a preheated broiler to let the cheese melt.

Meanwhile, cook the spaghetti in a pan of boiling water. Drain and serve on individual plates with the meatballs piled on top.

Party Sausages with Mustard and Honey Dip
SERVES 10-12

This is really fast and easy and can be served with the Homemade Pork Sausages on page 196, or with store-bought cocktail sausages if you are in a hurry and have a lot of little mouths to feed. The dip is slightly sweet from the honey, which works very well with the sausages. The Dijon mustard is not very hot, although you can add more mustard if you prefer and are serving to adults.

FOR THE SAUSAGES:
1 recipe Homemade Pork Sausages (see page 196) or 40 cocktail sausages

FOR THE DIP:
1 c crème fraîche
1 tbsp whole-grain mustard
1/2 tsp honey
1 tsp Dijon mustard

Cook the sausages in a frying pan, under the broiler or in a hot oven.

In a serving bowl, combine all of the dip ingredients. When the sausages are cooked, place the bowl of dip in the center of a large serving plate and arrange the sausages around.

Banana and Peanut Butter Muffins

MAKES 12 / VEGETARIAN

We all adore these muffins at home; they are sweet, delicious and nutty. They are also great for a snack or to take on a picnic. Put them in your kids' lunch boxes for a nice surprise!

2¼ c (10 oz) all-purpose flour
½ c (2 oz) rolled oats
1 tbsp baking power
2 eggs
⅔ c (5 oz) light brown sugar
2 bananas, peeled and mashed
½ c crunchy peanut butter
4 tbsp (½ stick) butter, melted
1 c milk

Preheat the oven to 375°F (190°C). Line a muffin pan with 12 paper muffin cups.

Place the flour, oats and baking powder in a bowl, mix together and set aside. In another bowl, whisk the eggs, add the light brown sugar, mashed bananas, peanut butter and the melted butter. Stir to mix, then add the milk and stir to combine. Add the dry ingredients and fold in gently; do not overmix.

Spoon the mixture into the muffin cups and bake for 18–24 minutes, or until the tops spring back when gently touched. Allow to stand in the muffin pan for a minute before turning out to cool on a wire rack.

Drop Scones

MAKES 12 / VEGETARIAN

These little drop scones (or crumpets) are quite delicious and are very easy to make. They are fabulous for brunch or for a quick snack in the afternoon. My children love making these after school when they are always a bit peckish.

1 c (4 oz) self-rising flour
1 tsp baking powder
2 tbsp superfine sugar
Pinch of salt
1 egg
1/2 c milk
Drop of sunflower oil, for greasing

Sift the flour and baking powder into a bowl, add the sugar and salt and stir to mix. Make a well in the center, crack in the egg and whisk, gradually drawing in the flour from the edge. Add the milk gradually, whisking all the time, to form a smooth batter.

Lightly grease a frying pan and warm it over a moderate heat. For each scone, drop 1 tablespoon of the batter into the pan, keeping the scones well apart so they do not stick together. Cook for about 2 minutes or until bubbles appear on the surface and begin to burst and the drop scones are golden underneath, then flip them over and cook on the other side for a minute or until golden on this side as well.

Remove from the pan and serve warm with butter and jam, apple jelly, Lemon Curd (see page 186) or, if you are like my children, chocolate spread! (If you wish, wrap the drop scones in a clean tea towel to keep warm while you make the rest.)

Chewy Seedy Oat and Apricot Bars

MAKES ABOUT 18 BARS / VEGETARIAN

Pack these in lunch boxes, but always be sure to steal one for yourself to enjoy with a cup of coffee once the kids have gone to school!

3⅓ c (11 oz) rolled oats
3/4 c (4 oz) pumpkin or sunflower
    seeds, or a mixture of the two
2/3 c (2 oz) shredded coconut
1/2 c (2 oz) all-purpose flour
14 tbsp (1¾ sticks) butter

1/2 c corn syrup
2/3 c (5 oz) light brown sugar
5 oz dried apricots, chopped
1/2 c crunchy peanut butter
1 tsp vanilla extract

Preheat the oven to 325°F (160°C). Line a 7 x 11-inch baking pan with nonstick baking parchment, leaving a little hanging over the edges for easy removal later.

Place the oats, seeds, coconut and flour in a large bowl and mix together. Melt the butter and corn syrup together in a saucepan, then mix in the sugar, chopped apricots, peanut butter and vanilla extract. Pour into the bowl of dry ingredients and mix until evenly combined.

Press the mixture into the prepared pan and bake in the oven for 20–25 minutes, or until golden and slightly firm. Allow to cool in the pan, then remove, still in the paper, and cut into 18 bars (or cut them whatever size you want them to be). Store in an airtight container for up to 1 week. These will also freeze well.

White Soda Scones

MAKES ABOUT 12 SCONES / VEGETARIAN

This has to be one of the fastest and most delicious scones you can make. The dough is just perfect for children to play around with, even if it does then get heavy from overhandling. You should see some of the creations that my sons make; dinosaurs are their favorites! This is the soda bread mixture we make at the Ballymaloe Cookery School, and there are countless variations you can experiment with from this basic recipe.

3²/₃ c (1 lb) all-purpose flour
1 tsp salt

1 tsp baking soda
1³/₄ c buttermilk or sour milk

Preheat the oven to 450°F (230°C). Sift the flour, salt and baking soda into a large bowl, and rub the mixture with your fingertips to incorporate some air. Make a well in the center and pour in most of the buttermilk. Using one hand, with your fingers open and stiff, mix in a full circle, bringing the flour and liquid together, adding more liquid if necessary. The dough should be quite soft, but not too sticky.

Turn it out onto a floured surface, and do not knead it but gently bring it into one ball. Flatten it slightly to a height of about 1¹/₂ inches. Cut the dough into squares or whatever shape you like. Put the scones onto a baking sheet, pop into the hot oven and cook for 10–15 minutes (depending on the size). Have a look at them after 10 minutes; if they are deep golden brown, then turn down the heat to 400°F (200°C) for the remainder of the time. When cooked they should sound hollow when tapped. Cool on a wire rack.

VARIATIONS

HERB SCONES

Add 1–2 tbsp of chopped fresh thyme, rosemary, parsley, chives, marjoram, savory or sage to the flour before you pour in the buttermilk. For even more flavor, you could sprinkle the tops with grated Cheddar cheese before they go into the oven.

PESTO SCONES

Add 1–2 tbsp basil pesto to the buttermilk before mixing with the flour. These are also delicious with chopped olives mixed in with the flour.

CRISPY BACON AND PARMESAN SCONES

Add about 1/3 cup chopped cooked crispy bacon, a good pinch of cayenne pepper and 2 oz finely grated Parmesan cheese to the flour at the start, then brush the tops of the raw scones with beaten egg or leftover buttermilk and sprinkle with more grated Parmesan cheese.

SWEET SCONES

Add 2 tbsp superfine sugar to the dry ingredients. Also, put 1 egg into a measuring cup, lightly beat and add buttermilk or sour milk to make 13/4 c. This makes the dough slightly richer. In addition, you could add any of the following ingredients to the flour at the start of the recipe: 4 oz golden raisins (or currants) and 1/2 teaspoon pumpkin pie spice; 4 oz chopped chocolate; or 1 teaspoon ground cinnamon and an extra 2 tbsp sugar. Then brush the tops with beaten egg and dip into 1/4 c (2 oz) granulated sugar mixed with 1/2 teaspoon ground cinnamon.

Jam Drops

MAKES ABOUT 30 / VEGETARIAN

These are quick little cookies, which makes them great to prepare with children since they won't lose their concentration halfway through. My boys love baking them!

1 2/3 c (7 oz) self-rising flour
1/2 c (4 oz) superfine sugar
8 tbsp (1 stick) slightly soft butter

1 small egg, beaten
Strawberry, raspberry or apricot jam

Preheat the oven to 375°F (190°C). In a food processor mix the flour, sugar and butter together. Add just enough egg to bring the mixture together to form a stiff dough. If you are not using a food processor, rub the butter into the flour and sugar, then add enough egg and with your hands work it until it forms a stiff dough.

Roll the mixture into balls the size of a walnut and place on a baking sheet (no need to line). Flatten each ball slightly and make a small indentation in the middle of each cookie with your thumb or the end of a wooden spoon. Drop half a teaspoon of jam in the center. Bake for 10–15 minutes until just golden. Cool on a wire rack.

5 Extended Family

My extended family not only includes relatives (grandparents, in-laws, aunts, uncles and cousins), it also includes those close friends and neighbors we know so well that they may as well be family! The food in this chapter is for all those easy, casual occasions when the whole gang gets together.

Winter Vegetable Broth with White Beans and Chorizo

SERVES 6

This soup is the best thing in wintertime—comforting and nutritious. It's a meal in itself for lunch. And, even better, it's very easy to make.

2 tbsp olive oil
1 onion, peeled and chopped
1 large carrot, peeled and chopped
2 small leeks, trimmed and chopped
2 potatoes, peeled and chopped
2 large garlic cloves, peeled and crushed

5 oz chorizo, sliced about 1/8 in thick
3 3/4 c chicken stock
One 15-oz can navy or cannellini beans, drained
2 tbsp chopped fresh cilantro or parsley
Salt and freshly ground black pepper

Heat the olive oil in a large saucepan. Add the onion, carrot, leeks, potatoes, garlic and chorizo. Cover and sweat for 10 minutes over a low heat, stirring every now and then.

Add the chicken stock and drained beans. Bring to the boil and simmer for 5 minutes until all the vegetables are cooked. Add the herbs, season to taste and serve.

Light Coconut Broth with Bok Choy and Basil
SERVES 8

I absolutely love this kind of recipe: you throw a few things in a pot, boil for a few minutes and end up with the most delicious result. I also adore these Southeast Asian flavors.

2½ quarts vegetable (or light chicken) stock
Two 13½-oz cans coconut milk
2 red chiles, deseeded and finely sliced into rings
4 scallions, trimmed and sliced thinly at an angle
2 garlic cloves, peeled and crushed
2 heaped tsp grated ginger
4 heads bok choy, stalk and leaves shredded
6 tbsp Thai fish sauce (nam pla)
Juice of 1 lime
¼ c sliced basil

Place the stock, coconut milk, chile, scallions, garlic and ginger in a saucepan and bring up to the boil. Add the bok choy and continue cooking for 1–2 minutes or until the bok choy is just cooked. Add the fish sauce, lime juice and basil. You probably won't need any additional salt since the fish sauce is already quite salty. Serve in warm bowls.

VARIATION
LIGHT COCONUT BROTH WITH BOK CHOY AND SHRIMP
Add 32 peeled tiger or other large shrimp into the broth with the shredded bok choy and cook as above. The shrimp will cook in the same time as the bok choy.

Chicken Pie with Ham and Peas

SERVES 8-10

My husband, Isaac, is an amazing cook, and this is one of his best weekend lunch dishes. It is so good and children love it too.

FOR THE FILLING:

1 chicken, about 5 lb
2 carrots, peeled and halved
1 celery stick, halved
1 onion, peeled and halved
Sprig of fresh thyme and fresh parsley
4¼ c water or light chicken stock
Salt and freshly ground black pepper
1 c light cream
Roux (see page 215)
2 tbsp butter
1 lb button mushrooms,
   cut in half

1 lb cooked ham, chopped
   into ¾-in cubes
1 lb green peas (fresh or frozen)
6 eggs, hard boiled for 10 minutes,
   peeled and chopped roughly
2 tbsp chopped fresh tarragon

FOR THE TOPPING:

14 oz puff pastry,
   rolled to ¼ in thick
1 egg, beaten, to glaze
Or
3¾ lb potatoes

Remove any giblets from inside the chicken and discard. Place the whole chicken in a large saucepan or casserole pot, add the carrots, celery, onion, thyme and parsley and the water or light chicken stock. Season with salt and pepper, cover with a lid and simmer for about 1¼ hours (or pop into a moderate oven) until the chicken is cooked. You will know when it is cooked as the leg will feel quite loose when you pull it from the carcass and the juices run clear when pierced.

If you have a pastry topping, preheat the oven to 450°F (230°C). For mashed potato, preheat the oven to 350°F (180°C).

Take the chicken out of the pot and set aside to cool for a few minutes. Remove the vegetables and herbs from the liquid in the pot and pour in the cream. Bring up to the boil, then whisk in some roux (about 2-3 tablespoons, but start with 1 tablespoon) until it has thickened slightly. The liquid must keep boiling while you add the roux in order to thicken.

Heat the butter in a pan over a high heat and fry the mushrooms for 4 minutes or until soft.

Remove the meat from the chicken carcass, chop roughly and place in a large baking dish (about 10 x 14 inches), then add the chopped ham, peas (these can be straight from the freezer), chopped hard-boiled eggs, browned mushrooms and the chopped tarragon. Season to taste. If you are making this in advance, don't add the topping until just before you're ready to cook.

For a puff pastry top: cut the pastry to the same size as the top of the baking dish and arrange on top, making a hole in the center to allow steam to escape. Brush the pastry with the beaten egg to give it a nice glaze. Cook it in the oven for 10 minutes, then turn down the oven to 375°F (190°C) and cook for another 20 minutes or until the pastry is golden brown and the mixture is bubbling hot.

For a mashed potato top: cook the potatoes and then mash them with a little bit of milk and butter and season with salt and pepper. Arrange the mashed potato on top of the chicken mixture and lightly score the surface. Place in the oven and cook for 30–40 minutes or until golden brown on top and bubbling hot.

Roast Leg of Lamb with Garlic and Rosemary and Olive Paste

SERVES 8-10

I love it when Isaac makes this for Sunday lunch. You can also serve it with Mint Sauce or Red Currant Jelly (see pages 216 and 217).

FOR THE LAMB:
1 leg of lamb, 5¹/₂-7¹/₄ lb
2 tbsp olive oil
1 tsp cracked black pepper (best if it is still a little coarse)
1 generous tbsp chopped fresh rosemary
1 big pinch of sea salt
8 garlic cloves, peeled and sliced

FOR THE OLIVE PASTE:
¹/₂ c (4 oz) pitted black olives
1 tbsp capers
1 tsp Dijon mustard
1 tsp freshly squeezed lemon juice
Freshly ground black pepper
¹/₄ c olive oil

Preheat the oven to 450°F (230°C). Using a very sharp knife, make about ten shallow slashes in criss-cross patterns on the top side of the meat. Mix together the olive oil, pepper, rosemary, sea salt and garlic and spread all over the lamb, pushing it into the incisions. Place it in a roasting pan and put it into the preheated oven.

Cook for 20 minutes, then turn the heat down to 350°F (180°C) and cook for a further 45 minutes for pink lamb, 1 hour 10 minutes for medium, or 1 hour 25 minutes for well-done. This cooking time allows 18 minutes per pound at this temperature. I usually aim for medium since there will inevitably be some pink bits and some well-done so that everyone can have their favorite!

To make the olive paste, whiz up the olives with the capers, mustard, lemon juice and pepper in a food processor—you probably won't need any salt. Add the olive oil and blend again. It keeps for months in a sterilized jar (see page 177) in the fridge.

When the lamb is cooked, allow it to rest for 15 minutes, covered with foil, somewhere warm if possible, then carve into slices and serve with the olive paste, mint sauce or red currant jelly.

Beef Stew with Brandy, White Wine and Cream

SERVES 10-12

This is such a good main course for entertaining; everyone always loves it. I usually make this quantity, even if I am feeding just six people, as it's useful having leftovers for the next day or two.

1 lb mushrooms, sliced
3-4 tbsp olive oil
7 lb stewing beef, cut into 1^1/$_2$-in cubes
^{2}/$_3$ c chicken or beef stock
3 very large onions, peeled and sliced
5 garlic cloves, peeled and crushed

^{2}/$_3$ c white wine
6 tbsp brandy
1^1/$_3$ c light cream
Salt and freshly ground black pepper
2-3 tsp Roux (see page 215)

Preheat the oven to 325°F (160°F). Heat a large frying pan and sauté the mushrooms in batches in the olive oil until pale golden in color. Tip onto a plate and set aside. Brown the meat in the same pan in small batches. When all the meat has browned, pour a small amount of the stock into the frying pan and bring to the boil to deglaze the pan and conserve the flavor.

Meanwhile, place a large flameproof casserole on the stove top over a medium heat and pour the stock from the frying pan into it. Add the mushrooms, meat, sliced onions, garlic, white wine, stock and brandy. Cover with the lid, transfer to the oven and simmer for about 1–1^1/$_2$ hours or until tender.

When the meat is cooked, strain the liquid into a saucepan. Add the cream and boil uncovered for a few minutes until it has a good flavor, then season with salt and pepper.

With the liquid still boiling, add 2–3 teaspoons of the roux and whisk in until the juices have thickened slightly, adding more roux if necessary. Pour over the meat, stir and keep warm until you are ready to serve. Serve with Pilaf Rice (see page 218) or mashed potatoes.

Spaghetti with Beef, Olives, Capers and Anchovies

SERVES 6-8

This is a really good and gutsy pasta dish adapted from the classic pasta puttanesca (whores' pasta!). Leave out the beef if you wish. The sauce can be made in advance.

3-4 tbsp olive oil
1¼ lb rump steak, cut into thin strips
2 onions, peeled and sliced
4 garlic cloves, peeled and crushed
One 14½-oz can chopped tomatoes or 1 lb fresh tomatoes, peeled (see page 178) and chopped, reserving the juice

Salt and freshly ground black pepper
Good pinch of sugar
2 tbsp chopped pitted black olives
2 tbsp whole capers, rinsed if salted
12 whole anchovy fillets, roughly chopped
2 tbsp chopped fresh tarragon or basil
1 lb 6 oz spaghetti

Heat half the olive oil in a pan, toss the meat for 30 seconds until brown, then remove from the pan and set aside. Add the remaining oil to the pan, and sweat the onion and garlic until soft. Add the tomatoes and their juices, salt and pepper and sugar. Cover with the lid and cook over a low heat for 10 minutes. Return the beef back to the sauce and allow it to simmer for a further 10 minutes or so until the sauce has thickened. Add the olives, capers, anchovies and chopped herbs, stir and set aside.

Cook the pasta in a large pot of boiling salted water until it is al dente. Drain and toss with the warm sauce and serve.

Gratin of Fish with Cheese, Tomatoes and Herbs

SERVES 6

Another great recipe of Isaac's! It is a terrifically easy and convenient main course and—even better—it can be prepared in advance.

3 oz Gruyère cheese, grated
3 oz Emmental, grated (or a total of 5 oz Gruyère instead)
1 generous tbsp Dijon mustard
4–5 tbsp light cream
Salt and freshly ground black pepper
18 cherry tomatoes
1 generous tsp fresh thyme leaves or 1½ tbsp torn basil
1½ lb filleted and skinned flat fish, such as flounder or lemon sole

Preheat the oven to 350°F (180°C). In a bowl, mix the grated cheese with the mustard and cream, add a twist of black pepper and set aside. Cut the cherry tomatoes in half, season with a little salt and sprinkle with the herbs.

Spread half the cheese mixture in a gratin dish (or individual ovenproof dishes). Lay half the fish on top, then add all the tomatoes and herbs. Add the second layer of fish, followed by the second layer of the cheese mixture. Place the dish in the fridge until you are ready to cook it.

Cook in the preheated oven for 20–30 minutes (or 15 minutes for single portions) until golden and bubbly. Serve with a big green salad and some boiled new potatoes if you wish.

VARIATION

This dish can also be made using round, fleshy fish, such as haddock or cod. Use the same weight as the flat fish but place just one layer of fish in the dish.

Chocolate and Hazelnut Toffee Tart

SERVES 8-10 / VEGETARIAN

This is a really special and divinely rich tart, which is perfect served at the end of a meal with a cup of espresso or a glass of sweet dessert wine. It looks fantastic with its layers of sweet biscuity pastry underneath the hazelnut toffee, topped off with a rich and intense chocolate mousse.

**1 recipe Sweet Shortcrust Pastry
(see page 221)**

FOR THE HAZELNUT TOFFEE:

4 tbsp (½ stick) butter

⅓ c light cream

½ c (4 oz) light brown sugar

**5 oz hazelnuts, roasted, peeled and
coarsely chopped**

FOR THE CHOCOLATE MOUSSE:

¾ c light cream

**7 oz dark chocolate, broken
into pieces**

TO SERVE:

Cocoa powder (optional)

Softly whipped cream

Roll out the pastry to line a 10-inch tart pan (see page 220 for instructions). Cover and chill for 20 minutes, then blind bake (see also page 220). The pastry will not go into the oven again, so it must be completely cooked.

For the hazelnut toffee layer, place the butter, cream and brown sugar in a saucepan, bring to the boil and simmer for 2–3 minutes until slightly thickened. Remove from the heat, add the hazelnuts and allow it to cool. Spread over the cooked tart shell.

For the chocolate mousse, place the cream in a saucepan and bring to the boil, remove from the heat and immediately add the chocolate, stirring until the chocolate has melted and mixed with the cream. It should be just tepid now. Pour over the hazelnut toffee in the pastry shell.

Place the tart somewhere cool until the chocolate mousse has set. If you are keeping it in the fridge, let it come back up to room temperature before you serve. Dust the tart with cocoa (if using), slice and serve with softly whipped cream.

Crème Brûlée au Café

FILLS 4-5 ESPRESSO CUPS, SHOT GLASSES OR SMALL RAMEKINS / VEGETARIAN

Not many recipes come into my head as I sleep (unfortunately), but I woke up one morning having dreamt that I had eaten this in Italy. So when I tried it out later that day, I was delighted with the result! It's an excellent dessert to round off a dinner party. The flavor of the coffee-infused custard is perfect with the burnt sugar topping: divine inspiration! For the caramel topping you can use superfine, granulated, light brown or dark brown sugar, but I have recommended light brown because the rich flavor works very well with the coffee custard. Since it is so rich it's best served in small portions. The custard needs to be made at least 5 hours in advance for it to set and be able to support the caramelized sugar top.

FOR THE CUSTARD:
1 generous tbsp ground coffee (not instant)
1 c heavy cream
2 egg yolks
1 tbsp light brown sugar
FOR THE CARAMELIZED TOPPING:
½ c (4 oz) light brown sugar

Place the coffee in a saucepan with the cream, bring up to just under boiling, then take off the heat and set aside for 1 minute to allow the coffee flavor to infuse. Pour through a very fine sieve into a bowl and wash out the saucepan.

Place the egg yolks and sugar in a bowl and whisk. Still whisking, add the coffee cream and mix completely. Pour this back into the clean, cool saucepan and place over a low heat. Stirring all the time, cook very slowly (it must not boil, otherwise it may scramble) until it thickens and can coat the back of a spoon—this will take a few minutes. Pour it immediately into serving cups, glasses or bowls and allow to cool, then place in the fridge for at least 5 hours (or overnight). Be careful not to break the skin on top or the caramel may sink later.

To prepare the caramel topping, place the sugar in a small saucepan over a medium heat and allow the sugar to caramelize, stirring all the time with a wooden spoon. It will look very lumpy and strange at first, but it will suddenly appear smooth, liquid and glossy. Immediately drizzle this caramel over the top of the custards. I like the custards to be just partially covered with the caramel. Do not swirl the custards while the caramel is being drizzled over as the skin may break and cause the caramel to sink. If using this method, the caramel can be made and poured on top of the custards about 5 or 6 hours in advance. Keep it somewhere dry so the caramel will not soften.

RACHEL'S HANDY TIP

If you have a cook's blowtorch, you can sprinkle the set custards with a layer of sugar, about ½–1 teaspoon per portion. Light your blowtorch and caramelize the sugar by holding the blowtorch just a few inches from the cups until the sugar melts and bubbles. Allow to sit for 1 minute before serving. These can be finished a couple of hours before serving.

Amaretti Cookie Ice Cream with Hot Mocha Sauce

SERVES 6 / VEGETARIAN

This is the perfect dessert for the person who doesn't like to make either pastry or cakes. It's also great if you're in a hurry and want to make something fabulous with minimum effort. I love the rich, intense chocolate sauce with a hint of coffee and, if you like, you can leave out the brandy. The sauce can be prepared in advance (it will keep pretty much indefinitely in the fridge); just heat gently to serve.

FOR THE ICE CREAM:
1 pint vanilla ice cream
4 oz amaretti cookies,
    broken into chunks

FOR THE HOT MOCHA SAUCE:
4 oz chocolate, chopped
6 tbsp good strong coffee (can be left
    over from that morning!)
1 tbsp brandy (optional)

Take the ice cream out of the freezer and allow it to soften slightly, then add the broken amaretti cookies and fold into the ice cream. Cover and put back in the freezer until you are ready to serve.

To make the hot mocha sauce, melt the chocolate in a heatproof bowl in a low oven or microwave, or in a bowl set over a pan of simmering water. Take off the heat and whisk in the coffee and the brandy, if using. Place a scoop or two of ice cream in a bowl, glass or cup and drizzle generously with the hot mocha sauce.

Little Hot After-Dinner Shots

MAKES 8 / VEGETARIAN

Merrilees Parker, who is a great cook, made something similar to these when I appeared with her on *Great Food Live*. These are like little Irish coffees, only without the coffee!

1 c brandy or whiskey
1 c Sugar Syrup (see page 221)
½ c (8 tbsp) softly whipped cream

Place the brandy or whiskey in a saucepan with the sugar syrup and heat very gently; do not boil. Divide between eight little glasses. Dip a spoon into boiling water and spoon a tablespoon of cream into each glass, allowing it to slide off the spoon and sit on top of the sweet brandy or whiskey. The cream should not sink. Serve immediately.

6 Dining Alfresco

I absolutely adore eating alfresco.
You just can't beat gorgeous, lazy
days out in the garden with friends
and family, fun barbecues, a lunch
under an umbrella for shade, enjoying
breakfast while listening to the birds
and smelling the roses, romantic
candlelit meals under the stars . . .
how lovely! I eat outdoors whenever
I get the chance, so that I can make
the most of our fairly brief but
warm summers.

Summer Omelette with Crispy Bacon, Tomato and Arugula Salad

SERVES 6

This is very much like an Italian frittata, with a gorgeous salad on top. It looks very pretty and dramatic on the table.

FOR THE OMELETTE:

4 tbsp olive oil
1 onion, peeled and chopped
Salt and freshly ground black pepper
8 eggs
1/3 c heavy cream
1/3 c milk
4 oz Gruyère or Parmesan cheese, grated
1-2 tbsp snipped fresh chives

FOR THE SALAD:

8 slices bacon, cooked until golden and crispy
6 ripe tomatoes, chopped into large chunks
1 tbsp olive oil
1-2 tsp lemon juice
Salt, freshly ground black pepper and sugar
2 oz arugula leaves (2 big handfuls)

Make the omelette first. Heat an 11-inch frying pan, add 2 tablespoons olive oil and the chopped onion, season and cook for 5-8 minutes, until almost soft and a little golden. Remove from the heat and allow to cool for a minute.

Whisk the eggs in a large bowl, add the cream, milk, the cooked onions, grated cheese and chopped chives; season to taste. Wipe out the frying pan, then heat it again and add the remaining 2 tablespoons olive oil, swirl it around, then pour in the egg mixture. Stir a couple of times, cook over a low heat until it is golden and set underneath (about 10-15 minutes), then place under a hot broiler to set the top (this may take another 4-5 minutes).

When cooked, flip or slide the omelette onto a large plate and set aside while you prepare the salad. It needs to cool slightly and to be eaten at room temperature.

To make the salad, slice the cooked bacon into 1/2-inch pieces. Place in a bowl, add the tomatoes and drizzle with the olive oil and the lemon juice; season with salt, pepper and a pinch of sugar. When you are ready, toss the arugula in very gently, then place on top of the omelette and serve.

This salad is also delicious made with smoked mackerel instead of the crispy bacon. Use 2-3 fillets of skinned smoked mackerel, cut into slices.

Asparagus Soldiers with Softly Boiled Eggs

SERVES 4 / VEGETARIAN

I love dipping spears of asparagus into softly boiled eggs, and they are great served up for an outdoor brunch. Do make sure you don't overcook the eggs or it will be tricky to dip the asparagus into the yolk!

4 eggs
12 asparagus spears, woody ends
   snapped off
Salt

Bring two saucepans of water up to the boil, one for the eggs and one for the asparagus. Boil the eggs in their shells for 4 minutes. While the eggs are boiling, cook the asparagus by dropping it into boiling water with a pinch of salt, cover and bring back up to the boil, then remove the lid and boil, uncovered, for 3–4 minutes until it is just cooked. Drain the eggs and the asparagus.

To eat, break open the "lid" of your boiled egg and dip the asparagus spears into the runny yolk.

Onion and Blue Cheese Tart

SERVES 6-8 / VEGETARIAN

Combined with a big green salad, this tart is perfect for an alfresco lunch in the garden. It is nice and easy to make, too, and there is no need to prebake the pastry.

FOR THE PASTRY:
2 c (9 oz) all-purpose flour
9 tbsp (1 stick plus 1 tbsp) butter
Pinch of salt
1 egg, beaten

FOR THE FILLING:
1/4 c olive oil
3 very large onions, peeled and sliced
2 sprigs of fresh thyme or rosemary
Salt and freshly ground black pepper
4 oz blue cheese, crumbled
   roughly into 1/2-in pieces

Make the pastry following the method on page 220 and allow it to rest in the fridge. Meanwhile, place the olive oil in a saucepan and add the sliced onions, herbs and salt and pepper. Stir, put on the lid and cook over a low heat for about 20 minutes, stirring regularly, until the onions are soft and tender. Discard the herb sprigs and pour out onto a plate to cool.

Roll out the chilled pastry between two sheets of plastic wrap. When it is big enough to line a 10-inch round tart pan, remove the top layer of plastic and flip the pastry into the pan with the remaining sheet of plastic on top. Press it into the edges of the pan, remove the plastic and trim the edges. Using a fork, prick holes into the base of the pastry shell. If you have time, it is best to allow the pastry to cool again before it goes into the oven to cook, so pop it into the freezer for 5 minutes if possible.

Preheat the oven to 350°F (180°C). Place a baking sheet in the oven to heat up (this will help the base of the tart cook more evenly).

Pour the onions into the chilled pastry shell, place on the hot baking sheet in the oven and cook for 25–35 minutes until the pastry around the edge is crisp and golden. About 3 minutes before the end of the cooking time, sprinkle the tart with the crumbled blue cheese and pop back into the oven for another 3 minutes. The blue cheese will just begin to melt. Remove the tart from the oven and allow to cool slightly before sliding out onto a serving plate.

Spring Greens Soup

SERVES 6-8 / VEGETARIAN

This soup can also be served cold, like the Green Leaf and Pea Soup (see page 120), and with a little swirl of crème fraîche or thick natural yogurt in the center.

2 tbsp butter
1 potato, peeled and chopped
1 onion, peeled and chopped
Salt and freshly ground black pepper
2½ c vegetable (or chicken) stock

2½ c milk (add some light cream
   to this if you wish)
8 oz spring greens, such as
   spinach, kale, or watercress,
   roughly chopped

Melt the butter in a saucepan, add the potatoes and onions, and season with salt and pepper. Cover and sweat on a gentle heat for 10 minutes, stirring every now and then. Take off the lid, add the stock and milk and bring to the boil. Cook until the potatoes are soft.

Add the greens and boil, uncovered, over a high heat for just 2–3 minutes until the greens have wilted. Do not overcook this soup or it will lose its fresh green color and flavor. As soon as it is cooked, puree it. Taste and correct the seasoning and serve.

Crab and Avocado Salad

SERVES 3-4

Not only is this a delicious salad, it is also great as a sandwich filling between two slices of really good brown or white bread.

7 oz cooked crabmeat
1 tbsp Dijon mustard
1 tbsp Mayonnaise (see page 216)
2 tbsp chopped watercress

1 tbsp torn basil
1 ripe avocado, peeled,
    stoned and diced
Salt and freshly ground black pepper

Mix all the ingredients together and season to taste. Place on a lettuce leaf on a plate to serve for a starter or, if eating as a light main course, enjoy with some green salad and some bread on the side.

Avocado, Orange and Watercress Salad

SERVES 6 / VEGETARIAN

This salad has wonderful fresh flavors. It's great with spicy food, like South American Beef Steak with Chimichurri Salsa (see page 127). If you want to make this in advance, leave out the avocado and watercress until you are almost ready to serve.

1/4 c olive oil
Juice of 1/2 lime
Sea salt and freshly ground
    black pepper
1 orange, peeled and chopped

2 avocados, peeled, stoned
    and chopped roughly
6 oz watercress sprigs
    (about 6 handfuls)

In a bowl mix the olive oil and lime juice and season with sea salt and freshly ground black pepper. Add the chopped orange and avocado. Then gently toss in the watercress sprigs and serve.

Warm Pasta Salad with Herbs, Garlic and Arugula
SERVES 4-6

This is perfect for alfresco eating; fresh and light and wonderful eaten either hot or just slightly warm. Leave out the chile if you wish.

14 oz pasta, like farfalle (pasta bows)
2 tbsp butter
2 tbsp olive oil
4 cloves garlic, crushed or grated
1/2-1 red chile, deseeded and finely chopped (optional)
2 generous tbsp chopped fresh herbs (I use a mixture
   of parsley, chives, basil and thyme)
20 cherry tomatoes, quartered
2 big handfuls of arugula, left whole
Sea salt and freshly ground black pepper
2 oz grated Parmesan cheese

Bring a large saucepan of salted water to the boil, add the pasta, and cook until al dente.

While the pasta is cooking, heat the butter and olive oil in a saucepan, add the garlic and chile, and cook for about 20 seconds. Be careful not to burn the garlic.

Remove from the heat and add the chopped herbs, the quartered cherry tomatoes and the arugula (it will wilt a bit from the heat). Season to taste with sea salt and freshly ground black pepper. Toss with the grated Parmesan and serve hot, or allow to cool and serve at room temperature.

South American Beef Steak with Chimichurri Salsa

SERVES 6

The flavors in the salsa marry beautifully with the steak, which can be cooked on a barbecue, or in a frying pan or grill pan on the stovetop. It is delicious served with the Avocado, Orange and Watercress Salad (see page 123).

6 sirloin steaks, about 1/2 in thick

FOR THE MARINADE:

6 garlic cloves, peeled and finely chopped

1 red chile, deseeded and finely chopped

Juice of 1 orange

Juice of 1 lemon

2 tbsp chopped fresh parsley

6 tbsp olive oil

FOR THE CHIMICHURRI SALSA:

1 garlic clove, peeled and finely chopped

1 tbsp finely chopped scallion

1 tbsp white wine vinegar

1 pinch of dried chile flakes

2 tbsp chopped fresh cilantro

2 tbsp chopped fresh parsley

Juice of 1/2 lime

6 tbsp olive oil

Salt and freshly ground black pepper

Using a sharp knife, score the steaks 1/16 inch deep in a criss-cross pattern. Combine the ingredients for the marinade in a shallow glass or ceramic dish or strong plastic bag, add the beef and toss in the marinade. Then place in the fridge for at least 1 hour (or up to about 8 hours).

To make the salsa, combine all the ingredients in a bowl and season to taste with salt and pepper.

Heat a grill pan, frying pan or your barbecue until very hot. Remove the beef from the marinade and cook for about 3–4 minutes on each side or longer, depending on your taste. Reserve the marinade and use it to brush over the steaks during cooking. Transfer to serving plates, spoon over the chimichurri salsa, with more in a bowl on the side, and serve.

Fruity Cocktails

MAKES 2-4 / VEGETARIAN

These are all really refreshing cocktails to have on a summer's evening with friends.

CAMPARI AND GRAPEFRUIT FIZZ

5 tbsp Sugar Syrup (see page 221)
1 tbsp Campari
½ c grapefruit juice
3/4 c plus 2 tbsp sparkling white wine

Place the syrup, Campari and grapefruit juice in a pitcher and stir. Add the sparkling wine and pour into chilled champagne or wine glasses.

COOL CAMPARI AND LIME GIN AND TONIC

1/3 c gin
2 tbsp Campari
Juice of 1 lime (or ½ lemon)
3/4 c crushed ice
6 tbsp tonic water

Pour the gin, Campari and lime or lemon juice into a pitcher. Add the crushed ice, stir to mix, then add the tonic water. Serve in whiskey tumblers or strain into cocktail glasses.

STRAWBERRY OR RASPBERRY DAIQUIRI

2/3 c white rum or vodka
9 oz strawberries or raspberries (can be frozen)
1/3 c lime juice (approximately 3 limes)
6-8 tbsp (3½-4 fl oz) Sugar Syrup (see page 221), to taste
Crushed ice, to serve

Place the rum, strawberries (or raspberries), lime juice and 6 tablespoons sugar syrup in a blender and whiz until smooth. Taste and add more syrup if necessary. Pour into tumblers half-filled with crushed ice.

Baked Meringue with Peaches

SERVES 6 / VEGETARIAN

A past student at the cookery school, Jo Jessop, who comes from South Highlands, Australia, gave me this recipe. It's wonderful served with vanilla ice cream; the hot baked meringue with the frozen ice cream works very well in that "baked Alaska" kind of way. It is just as easy to make this for 26 as it is for six, provided you have a large enough baking dish!

4 peaches or nectarines
2 tbsp light brown sugar
2 tbsp Marsala, sweet sherry or lemon juice
4 egg whites
1 c (9 oz) light brown sugar or superfine sugar

Preheat the oven to 350°F (180°C). Cut the peaches in half (there's no need to peel them) and remove the pits. Slice the peaches about 1/4 inch thick and lay in a 9-inch deep dish pie pan. Sprinkle with the 2 tablespoons of brown sugar and drizzle with the Marsala, sherry or lemon juice. If the peaches are not very ripe and juicy (although they should be ripe enough to eat), pop them into the oven for 5 minutes to cook while you make the meringue. If they are very ripe and juicy there is no need to do this.

To make the meringue, whisk the egg whites in a bowl with an electric beater until stiff. Still beating, gradually add the light brown sugar and continue to beat until the meringue holds stiff peaks. Spoon the meringue on top of the peaches and cook in the preheated oven for 15–20 minutes, or until the meringue feels slightly firm in the center and is a deep golden color on top.

7 Home Cinema

Cooking for an evening of home cinema is such fun. It is the perfect excuse to indulge and eat sticky, gooey treats in front of the telly, all snuggled up under a blanket watching your favorite flicks. The only trick is to make sure you either prepare food that can be eaten with your hands or food that is all on the one plate and not awkward to eat, or else you'll be forever picking bits off the sofa, your lap, or each other!

Baked Potatoes

SERVES AS MANY AS YOU LIKE / VEGETARIAN

A baked potato is the perfect food to eat while watching a good movie. Whether your favorite topping is baked beans or Manchego cheese with Serrano ham, there is always something in the fridge for everyone. Baked potatoes are good and wholesome because most of the goodness in a potato is stored just under the skin, which is retained when you bake it—none of it is lost in cooking water.

1 large potato per person in its skin, scrubbed clean

Preheat the oven to 450°F (230°C). Pierce a few holes in each potato with a skewer or a fork and put on a baking sheet or rack in the preheated oven. Cook for 40-55 minutes, until the potato feels soft under the crispy skin. You can cook the potatoes with a metal skewer stuck through them to speed up the cooking process. When the potato is baked, remove it from the oven and cut a cross in it to open it out slightly. Serve with a topping of your choice—each of those given here (turn the page for two more) makes enough for two potatoes.

SERRANO HAM AND MANCHEGO CHEESE WITH WALNUT DRESSING
2 slices Serrano ham (or Parma ham)
4 slices of Manchego cheese (or grated Parmesan cheese)
FOR THE WALNUT DRESSING:
1 tbsp walnut oil
1 generous tsp white wine vinegar
1/4 tsp Dijon mustard
Salt and freshly ground black pepper

Shake all the dressing ingredients together in a jar with a screw-top lid. Drape a slice of Serrano ham and a couple of thin slices of Manchego cheese over the top of each opened potato. Drizzle with a teaspoon or two of the walnut dressing.

GRUYÈRE CHEESE AND CRISPY BACON
2 tbsp chopped bacon
1 tbsp butter
¼ c grated Gruyère cheese
Freshly ground black pepper

Cook the bacon in a hot pan until crispy. Dot each potato with the butter, sprinkle with the crispy bacon, the grated cheese and a little black pepper, and pop it back into the hot oven for 3–4 minutes until the cheese is melted and bubbling.

SMOKED SALMON
2 oz smoked salmon (for 2 people)
1 tbsp capers, rinsed then dried in paper towels
1½ tsp butter or olive oil
Freshly ground black pepper
Squeeze of lemon juice
2 tbsp crème fraîche
Handful of snipped fresh chives

Cut the salmon into little strips and toss with the capers in the butter or olive oil in a hot pan. Add the pepper and a squeeze of lemon juice. Add a good tablespoon of crème fraîche onto the split cooked potatoes, sprinkle with the salmon and capers and decorate with chopped chives.

Yummy Dips

EACH DIP SERVES 4-6 PEOPLE / VEGETARIAN

I love having a selection of dips on a home-cinema night. Tortilla chips (bought, or homemade and baked) are great for dipping, as are roast potato wedges or even, dare I say, raw vegetable sticks (but only if I am feeling very good and virtuous). These dips can all be made in advance, and their individual flavors work well with each other.

HUMMUS

One 15-oz can chickpeas, drained,
  or 7 oz dried chickpeas
Juice of 1/2-1 lemon
2 garlic cloves, peeled and crushed
3-4 tbsp olive oil
2 generous tbsp tahini (sesame seed
  paste)
Salt and freshly ground black pepper
2 tbsp plain yogurt (optional)

If using dried chickpeas, soak them in water overnight, then drain and cook in fresh water for about 45 minutes, or until soft. Drain again and allow to cool. Put all the ingredients into a food processor and pulse until smooth. Check for seasoning, and add more olive oil or some yogurt, if using, if it is too thick. This keeps in the fridge for up to a week.

TOMATO AND CUCUMBER SALSA

16 cherry tomatoes, or 4 red ripe
  tomatoes, finely chopped
1/4 cucumber, deseeded and finely
  chopped
2 garlic cloves, peeled and crushed
1/2 small red onion, peeled and finely
  chopped
1-2 tbsp lemon or lime juice
1-2 tbsp chopped mint
Salt and freshly ground black pepper

Mix all the ingredients in a bowl and season to taste.

CRÈME FRAÎCHE WITH SWEET CHILI

6 tbsp crème fraîche
2 tbsp sweet chili sauce

Mix together the ingredients, adding more sweet chili sauce if you like.

Toasted Ham and Gruyère Sandwich

MAKES 1 SANDWICH

This is a classic combination, and I think it makes the ultimate TV supper. This recipe makes enough for one sandwich, but you can easily make more for a crowd!

2 slices of white bread, ciabatta or sourdough bread
Softened butter
2 slices of ham or, even better, bacon
2–3 slices of Gruyère cheese
1 tbsp whole-grain or Dijon mustard

Lay the slices of bread on a work surface. Spread one slice with butter, add a layer of ham, then the Gruyère cheese. Spread the other slice of bread with the mustard and place on top of the ham, mustard-side-down. Spread some butter on the top of the sandwich.

Place a frying pan on the heat and straight away put the sandwich in the pan, butter-side-down. Place a saucepan lid on the pan and cook over a medium heat for about 3–4 minutes, until golden on the underside. Spread a tiny bit of butter on the top and flip over. Cover again, turn down the heat and cook for another 3–4 minutes until golden and the cheese is just melted. Remove from the pan and serve.

RACHEL'S HANDY TIP

To make a lot of these I would cook the sandwiches in a hot oven for 8–10 minutes, which is far more convenient than cooking them one by one in a frying pan.

Lamb Samosas

MAKES 20

I love it when Isaac makes these for a night in front of the flicks. Samosas are the ultimate finger food, which makes them the ultimate telly food! Use filo pastry as a faster alternative to the traditional samosa pastry. For a vegetarian version, replace the lamb with an equal quantity of boiled, skinned and chopped potato.

2 tbsp sunflower or olive oil
3/4 lb finely chopped
   or minced lamb
1 onion, peeled and chopped
1 tsp ground cumin
1 tsp ground coriander

Salt and freshly ground black pepper
4 oz green peas (fresh or frozen)
1 tbsp chopped fresh cilantro
5 sheets of filo pastry, 10 x 20 in
1 egg, beaten

Heat a frying pan, add the sunflower or olive oil, then toss in the lamb, onion and ground spices. Season and cook for about 10 minutes without a lid until the lamb is just cooked and the juices have evaporated. Add the peas and toss. Take off the heat, add the chopped cilantro and season again to taste. Set aside for a minute to let the lamb cool.

Meanwhile, lay the filo pastry out on a board and cut in half vertically and horizontally, so you have four rectangles from each whole sheet. Cover all the pieces of filo with a barely damp tea towel (to prevent them from drying out). Place one sheet lengthwise in front of you and pile a heaping teaspoon of the lamb mixture at the end closest to you. Roll the pastry from the end closest to you once, then fold in both the long sides and then roll over and over, away from you, into a little parcel. Brush the finishing edge with a little of the beaten egg to seal and then place on a baking sheet. Brush the finished samosa with beaten egg and repeat with all the remaining pastry and meat.

These can be prepared earlier in the day up to this point and chilled in the fridge. To cook, place the baking sheet in an oven preheated to 425°F (220°C) for 10–12 minutes until golden.

Creamy Tomatoes on Toast

SERVES 2 / VEGETARIAN

My mum used to make this for us when we came home from school and I still adore it.
This is great, easy food to have in front of the television.

3/4 c light cream
1 sprig of fresh rosemary or 2 sprigs of fresh thyme
1 garlic clove, peeled and chopped
4 ripe tomatoes, cut in half
Sea salt and freshly ground black pepper
2–4 slices of white or wheat bread
About 2 tbsp olive oil

Preheat the oven to 400°F (200°C). In a saucepan, simmer the cream with the herbs and garlic for 5 minutes until it has thickened slightly.

Place the tomatoes cut-side-up in a gratin or ovenproof dish and pour the cream with garlic and herbs over them. Season with salt and pepper and then bake in the oven for 15–20 minutes or until the tomatoes are soft and blistered and the cream is thick and reduced.

Meanwhile, drizzle the bread with a little of the olive oil and pop into the oven for the last 5 minutes of the cooking time. When the toast and tomatoes are cooked, remove from the oven. Place the toast slices on warm plates and divide the tomato halves among them, then spoon any cream left in the gratin dish over the top and serve.

Raclette

SERVES 4

Raclette is both the name of a semi-soft Savoyard cheese and a traditional dish in which slices of the cheese were put on the hearth near a glowing fire. Diners would gather around with plates, knives and forks in hand and a bowl of boiled potatoes. As the cheese melted, it was scraped off, spread across the potatoes and eaten with gusto! Today, most people use electric raclette machines at the table and diners help themselves to cheese to melt on their own little handled tray under the raclette grill, which they then enjoy with hot boiled potatoes, a selection of charcuterie, cornichons and tomatoes. Similar to a cheese fondue, it's great fun for a big casual supper party, or amazing to enjoy in front of a good movie—set the raclette machine on a low coffee table near the sofa.

8–12 floury potatoes
1 lb Raclette cheese, cut into slices ¼ in thick
A selection of charcuterie
Ripe tomatoes
Cornichons, sliced
Cucumber Pickle (see page 174)
A chutney such as Spicy Tomato and Apple Chutney (see page 179) or Onion Marmalade (see page 181)
Sea salt and black pepper in a mill

Plug in the raclette machine and allow it to heat up. Boil the potatoes until soft.

Put the cheese, charcuterie, tomatoes, cornichons, cucumber pickle and relishes on plates or in bowls. When the potatoes have boiled, place them in a warm bowl on the table. Let each guest take a slice of cheese and place it under the grill on the raclette machine. While the cheese is melting, let everyone help themselves to all the other ingredients on the table. Split open a potato and when the cheese is melted and bubbling, scrape it onto the potato and enjoy.

Popcorn Paradise
SERVES 4 / VEGETARIAN

It is difficult to have a home-cinema night without popcorn, so why not try this recipe and all its variations? Serve the popcorn in a big bowl or in paper cornets for each person.

PLAIN POPCORN
3 tbsp sunflower oil
1/3 c popcorn kernels
2 tbsp butter
Pinch of salt

Heat the oil in a medium saucepan. Add the popcorn and swirl the pan to coat the popcorn in oil. Turn down the heat to low and cover; the corn should start to pop in a couple of minutes. As soon as it stops popping (after 5–7 minutes), take the saucepan off the heat and add the butter and salt. Put the lid back on the pan and shake to mix. Pour out into bowls and leave to cool a little.

VARIATIONS

TOFFEE POPCORN
Cook the popcorn as for the plain popcorn recipe, but while the corn is popping, make the toffee coating by melting 2 tablespoons butter in a small saucepan. Then add 2 tablespoons brown sugar and 1 generous tablespoon corn syrup and stir over a high heat for 1/2–1 minute until thick. Pour the toffee over the popcorn, put the lid on the pan and shake to mix. Pour out into bowls and cool a little before serving.

SPICED POPCORN
Cook the popcorn as for the plain popcorn recipe as far as removing the pan from the heat. In a bowl, mix 1 1/2 teaspoons each of ground cumin and coriander seeds with 1/2 teaspoon each of medium-strength curry powder and ground paprika and 3/4 teaspoon ground cayenne pepper. Heat 2 teaspoons sunflower oil in a frying pan, add the spices and stir for about 30 seconds until lightly toasted. Throw in 2 tablespoons superfine sugar and 3/4 teaspoon salt, stir, then add all of this into the popped popcorn in the saucepan, toss and empty into a big bowl.

8 Big Celebrations

From time to time we all find ourselves in a situation where we need to cook for lots of people—it could be for a big birthday or anniversary party, or maybe even an informal party after a wedding. On such occasions, the food needs to be something that can be prepared in advance, food that is easy to serve, and food with ingredients that everyone will like. To top it all, the food must also be just as easy to make for 26 as it is for 16 or even 6! So hopefully you'll find lots of inspiration in this chapter.

Green Salad with Honey Mustard Dressing

SERVES ABOUT 20 PEOPLE / VEGETARIAN

There can be nothing easier to prepare for a large gathering than a bowl filled with a beautiful combination of your favorite salad ingredients. A green salad doesn't have to be bland and uninteresting. It all depends on the leaves that you use (a good selection will give a lovely range of colors and flavors—try edible flowers too!), and the oil in the dressing. Try to use as good an olive oil as you can afford and it will make all the difference.

FOR THE GREEN SALAD:

As large a selection as possible of edible leaves and herbs
Edible flowers, such as wild garlic, nasturtium, edible chrysanthemum and chive

FOR THE DRESSING:

3 tbsp olive oil (use your best extra-virgin for this)
1 tbsp white wine vinegar
1 tsp whole-grain mustard
1 tsp honey
1 large garlic clove, peeled and crushed
Sprig of parsley
A few chives, trimmed and chopped
Salt and freshly ground black pepper

Wash and dry the leaves and flowers and then tear them into bite-sized pieces. Put into a plastic bag or a covered bowl, which can be stored in the fridge for a couple of days if you need to prep the greens in advance. This is particularly good if you buy or pick all your leaves in one go or you have friends staying for the weekend. You can then just pick and choose whatever you need, whenever you need it.

To make the dressing, place all the ingredients in a jar with a lid and shake to mix. Taste for seasoning. Drizzle sparingly over a selection of your prepared salad ingredients in a bowl and toss to serve.

Chicken Pilaf
SERVES 6

This is a great main course for feeding lots of people and can be made in advance. It's a firm favorite of adults and children alike. For large gatherings, double or triple the quantities.

1 large chicken, about 5½ lb
1 carrot, peeled and halved
1 onion, peeled and halved
6 whole black peppercorns
Large sprig of parsley
Large sprig of thyme

¾ c chicken stock
1 c white wine
Salt and freshly ground black pepper
1 c light cream
2-3 tbsp Roux (see page 215)

Preheat the oven to 325°F (160°C). Remove any giblets from the chicken carcass and place the chicken in a large saucepan or casserole. Add the carrot, onion, peppercorns, herbs, stock and white wine and bring up to the boil. Season with salt and pepper, cover with the lid and place in the preheated oven to cook for 1½-2 hours or until the chicken is completely cooked. I test this by pulling the leg—if it feels as though it will come away from the carcass easily and the juices run clear when pierced, then it is ready. (For a larger chicken, cook for 20 minutes per pound plus 30 minutes.)

Remove the chicken from the stock and place it on a large plate. Remove all the meat from the carcass, discarding the skin and bones. Cut the chicken into strips approximately ½ inch wide and 2 inches long. Cover and keep warm.

Remove the vegetables, peppercorns and herbs from the liquid and discard. Add the cream, bring up to the boil and boil uncovered for a few minutes. If the flavor is a little weak, boil for longer, then season to taste. While still boiling, whisk in the roux—you need enough to thicken it so it just about coats the back of a spoon.

Place the chicken and any juices back in the casserole, once again correcting the seasoning, and keep warm until needed. Serve with Pilaf Rice (see page 218), mashed potatoes or boiled new potatoes and the Green Salad with Honey Mustard Dressing (see page 150).

Moroccan Lamb Tagine with Lemon and Pomegranate Couscous

SERVES 12-14

This is one of those great dishes that is perfect for small dinner parties and big celebrations alike. It's very straightforward to prepare and is so, so delicious!

¼ c olive oil
8 garlic cloves, peeled and crushed
4 onions, peeled and chopped
4 tsp grated ginger
1½ tbsp coriander seeds, crushed
1 tbsp cumin seeds, crushed
1 tbsp ground cinnamon
Salt and freshly ground black pepper
7 lb shoulder of lamb, boned, fat discarded and cut into 1½-in cubes
2 tbsp tomato paste

4½ lb ripe tomatoes or four 14½-oz cans tomatoes, coarsely chopped
4-5 tbsp honey
Wedges of lime and a bowl of Greek yogurt, to serve

FOR THE COUSCOUS:

1 large or 2 small pomegranates
1¾ lb couscous
6 tbsp olive oil
Juice of 2 lemons
4¼ c boiling chicken stock or water
¼ c chopped fresh mint or cilantro

Preheat the oven to 325°F (160°C). Heat a large flameproof casserole or heavy saucepan, and add the olive oil, garlic, onions, ginger and spices. Season with salt and pepper, stir and cook on a low heat with the lid on for about 10 minutes, until the onions are soft.

Add the lamb, tomato paste, chopped tomatoes and honey. Stir it all together, bring to a simmer, cover and place in the oven for 1½ hours, until the lamb is tender and cooked. Remove the lid halfway through cooking to let the liquid reduce and thicken. Season to taste. If it is still a bit thin, put the dish or saucepan on the stove on a medium heat and without the lid. Stir occasionally and let the liquid thicken.

Cut the pomegranate in half. Scoop out the seeds using a teaspoon and remove the white membrane. Place the couscous in a bowl and mix in the olive oil and lemon juice. Pour in the boiling stock or water and season. Allow to sit in a warm place for 5-10 minutes until the liquid is absorbed. To serve, stir in the chopped herbs and pomegranate seeds. Place the tagine on serving plates with couscous and a wedge of lime, and place a bowl of thick yogurt in the middle of the table.

Thai Pork with Coconut Cilantro Sauce

SERVES 10-12

This is a delicious recipe with mild Southeast Asian flavors. The dish keeps very well if you make it in advance; just keep the cooked pork in a saucepan with the sauce, which will prevent the meat from drying out. Heat it up gently when you're ready to serve it.

4¹⁄₂ lb pork tenderloin, trimmed

FOR THE MARINADE:

¹⁄₄ c roughly chopped fresh cilantro leaves and stalks

10 scallions, trimmed

1¹⁄₄-in piece of fresh ginger, peeled and chopped

8 garlic cloves, peeled

Finely grated zest of ¹⁄₂ lemon

1 red chile, deseeded and roughly chopped

2 stalks of lemongrass, trimmed and outer leaves discarded

¹⁄₄ c light brown sugar

¹⁄₄ c soy sauce

¹⁄₄ c fish sauce (nam pla)

¹⁄₄ c sesame oil

FOR THE SAUCE:

Two 13¹⁄₂-oz cans coconut milk

2 tbsp fish sauce (nam pla)

2 tbsp lemon juice

1-2 tbsp chopped fresh cilantro leaves and stalks

Salt and freshly ground black pepper

Cut the pork at an angle into slices ¹⁄₂ inch thick, so that you have oval slices about 4 inches long and 2¹⁄₂ inches wide.

Make the marinade by placing the cilantro, scallions, ginger, garlic, lemon zest, chile and lemongrass in a food processor and whiz until you have a fine paste. Put into a bowl and add the remainder of the marinade ingredients. (If using a blender, simply blend all the marinade ingredients together.) Add the slices of pork and toss in the marinade. Cover and place in the fridge until you are ready to cook the meat (for at least 30 minutes, or even overnight if you wish).

Heat a frying pan or grill pan until it is almost smoking, remove the pork from the marinade (reserving the marinade for the sauce) and cook the pork in a single layer over a high heat for 1-2 minutes or until golden underneath. Turn and continue to cook until the meat is cooked through. If you are cooking lots of meat, you can just toss for 1 minute on each side in the pan, then transfer it to a roasting pan and cook in a hot oven preheated to 425°F (220°C) for another 5 minutes or until it is cooked through.

While the pork is cooking, place the reserved marinade in a small saucepan. Add the coconut milk, bring up to the boil and boil uncovered for about 5 minutes until it has thickened a little. Add the fish sauce, lemon juice and chopped cilantro and season to taste with more fish sauce or lemon juice if necessary. The fish sauce is quite salty so you might not need any additional salt.

Serve the pork on a bed of Thai Rice (see page 219) or Plain Boiled Rice (see page 218) with some sauce on top or in a bowl on the side.

RACHEL'S HANDY TIP

This main course also works very well as a canapé. Just cut the pork into small cubes about 3/4 inch square and thread onto cocktail sticks (or small satay sticks) that have been soaking in water for 1 hour. Cook on a barbecue or in a frying pan for 6 minutes on each side and serve with a bowl of the coconut cilantro sauce in the center of the plate.

Thai Stir-Fried Beef with Red Peppers and Bok Choy
SERVES 16

This is a great stir-fry that can be prepped in advance and then cooked when you are nearly ready to serve. I love to serve this with noodles or rice and some wedges of lime for each person to squeeze over his or her own plateful.

5¼ lb rump or sirloin steak, trimmed and thinly sliced across the grain
½ c fish sauce (nam pla)
½ c oyster sauce
8 large garlic cloves, peeled and chopped
½ c sunflower oil or vegetable oil
6 large red peppers, quartered, deseeded and finely sliced
8 heads bok choy, root end trimmed, then sliced across about ½ in thick
4-6 small chiles, deseeded and chopped
½ c roughly chopped basil (don't chop until you need it as it goes black if chopped in advance)
Lime wedges, to serve

Place the sliced beef in a bowl and add half the fish sauce, half the oyster sauce and half the chopped garlic. Stir to mix and leave to marinate, covered, in the fridge for 1–2 hours if possible, or even longer if you can.

Heat half the oil in a wok (or large frying pan), add the red pepper and toss over the heat for a couple of minutes, then add the bok choy. Keep tossing over the heat until just tender, then add the remaining garlic and the chiles. Cook for another 10 seconds, then remove from the heat and set aside.

Heat the remaining oil in the wok or pan, and when it is very hot, add the beef, drained from any marinade (reserve the marinade for later). Cook for 2 minutes, stirring all the time, or until cooked through.

Return the vegetables to the wok, add the remaining fish sauce, oyster sauce and marinade and bring to a boil for 30 seconds. Taste and add more fish sauce and oyster sauce if you wish. Remove from the heat and stir in the roughly chopped basil, and serve immediately with a wedge of lime on the side of each plate and with steamed rice or noodles.

Beef with Prunes and Peppers

This recipe from my friend Iona Murray is absolutely great for serving lots of people. It is best made several hours in advance or even the day before, which makes it very handy for entertaining. The prunes seem to dissolve and give the sauce a sweet richness.

8 lb chuck/stewing beef, trimmed
   and cut into 3/4-in chunks
3-4 tbsp olive oil
Salt and freshly ground black pepper
3 large onions, peeled and chopped
6 fat garlic cloves, peeled
One 750-ml bottle of red wine
8-10 red peppers, deseeded
   and chopped
Large bunch of thyme, tied together

3-4 fresh bay leaves
12 oz pitted ready-to-eat prunes,
   cut in half
Zest of 1 large orange, thinly sliced, and
   juice from the orange
4 red chiles, deseeded and chopped
1/4 c tomato paste
1 cinnamon stick
Roux (see page 215) (optional)

Preheat the oven to 325°F (160°C). Trim the meat and put it in a large bowl. Drizzle with 1-2 tablespoons of the olive oil and season with salt and pepper.

Heat a frying pan over a high heat and brown all the meat in batches. Remove the meat from the pan and place in a large saucepan or casserole. Add some more olive oil to the pan and toss the onions and garlic on a high heat for a minute, then transfer to the casserole. With the frying pan still on the heat, pour some of the wine into it and stir around for a minute; this will deglaze the frying pan. Pour into the casserole.

Add the peppers, thyme, bay leaves, prunes, orange zest and juice, the chiles, the remaining wine, the tomato paste and the cinnamon stick; mix again and bring to the boil. Season and cover with a well-fitting lid and place in the oven. Cook for about 2 hours, until the meat is meltingly tender and you can cut it with a fork. If it is looking dry, add some water or light stock.

When it is done, remove from the oven and allow to cool. Remove thyme, bay leaves and cinnamon stick. If the sauce is too runny, put a ladleful in a small saucepan, bring to the boil and whisk in some roux, return to the main dish and mix in. Or if the sauce is too dry, add a bit of stock or water to get the desired consistency. Serve with rice or mashed potatoes.

Roast Southeast Asian Salmon

SERVES 12-15

This is such a great main course for a big dinner party or family gathering.

2 fresh salmon fillets, each weighing
   2-2½ lb
Salt and freshly ground black pepper
FOR THE SAUCE:
⅔ c fish sauce (nam pla)
⅔ c white wine

2 garlic cloves, peeled and crushed
1 tbsp finely grated ginger
2 tbsp light brown sugar
Juice of 2 small limes
1 handful chopped fresh cilantro

Preheat the oven to 400°F (200°C). Place the fish, skin-side-down, on an oiled piece of tin foil on a baking sheet. Fold up the edges slightly to make a wall around the fish and season with salt and pepper.

Mix together the fish sauce, white wine, garlic, ginger and brown sugar in a saucepan and boil uncovered for about 5 minutes or until slightly thickened. Pour half of the sauce over the fish and cook in the oven for 20 minutes, or until the fish is cooked.

When the fish is cooked, transfer to a serving plate. Add the lime juice and chopped cilantro to the remaining sauce and spoon over the hot salmon. Serve with noodles or rice. This dish is also delicious served at room temperature with salads.

Vietnamese Crab Salad with Rice Noodles

SERVES 8-10 AS A STARTER

This is a really gorgeous and substantial salad and I absolutely adore these sweet, salty Southeast Asian flavors.

FOR THE DRESSING:

1/2 c (4 oz) sugar, or more to taste
6 tbsp fish sauce (nam pla)
6 tbsp lemon or lime juice (juice of
    2 lemons or about 3 limes)
2-3 small chiles, deseeded and
    sliced finely
4 garlic cloves, peeled and crushed
1 tbsp finely grated ginger

FOR THE SALAD:

9 oz thin or medium rice noodles
5 oz peanuts
1 lb cooked crabmeat
1 large cucumber, chopped
11 oz radishes, trimmed and sliced
1/4 c roughly chopped fresh cilantro
    leaves and stalks

To make the dressing, mix all the ingredients in a pitcher. Put the noodles in a bowl of boiling water for 5 minutes until they have softened. Drain and rinse. Meanwhile, toast the peanuts under the broiler preheated to hot. Rub off the skins and roughly chop the nuts.

In a bowl, toss together the dressing with the noodles, then add the crabmeat, chopped cucumber and sliced radishes. Sprinkle the toasted peanuts and the cilantro over the top and serve.

VARIATION

CRUNCHY VIETNAMESE SALAD WITH RICE NOODLES

Replace the crab with 4 oz each of bean sprouts, watercress and grated carrot.

Sicilian Pasta

SERVES 16-20 / VEGETARIAN

I first tasted this when a friend, James Folks, made it for a group of us, sitting outside on a hot summer's day drinking Prosecco, and it was absolutely divine. It is essential to make the marinade at least 2 hours in advance so that the vegetables almost soften and the flavors infuse.

FOR THE MARINADE:
4 large handfuls torn fresh basil
16 celery stalks, trimmed and finely chopped
16 garlic cloves, peeled and chopped
20 ripe tomatoes, chopped, or 50-60 cherry tomatoes, quartered
2/3 c olive oil
1½ lbs buffalo mozzarella, finely chopped
Sea salt and freshly ground black pepper
FOR THE PASTA:
4 lb small pasta shapes, such as fusilli

Place all the marinade ingredients in a bowl and season to taste. Leave to sit for at least 2 hours or longer if possible; do not put it in the fridge.

Once the marinade is ready, cook the pasta in a large pot of salted water and drain. Immediately toss with the marinade ingredients—the mozzarella will just begin to melt. Tip into a large serving bowl and place in the middle of the table. This dish is best eaten just warm.

Pasta with Garlic, Anchovies and Breadcrumbs
SERVES 12-15

This very simple peasant pasta dish originates from Naples. It's quick and very delicious.

6 oz fresh breadcrumbs
1 c olive oil
2 tsp dried chile flakes
Two 2-oz cans anchovy fillets, drained
and roughly chopped

1 head garlic, separated into cloves,
peeled and roughly chopped
4 lb spaghetti or tagliatelle
Juice of 1 lemon

Put the breadcrumbs in a dry frying pan and toss over a medium to high heat for a minute or two until they are golden, then set aside. Place the olive oil, chile flakes, anchovies and garlic in the frying pan over a medium to high heat for about 30 seconds (just long enough for the garlic to lose its rawness). Take off the heat and throw in the breadcrumbs to stop the cooking, and set aside.

Cook the pasta in a pot of boiling salted water, until al dente, then drain, leaving a couple of tablespoons of the cooking water in with the pasta. Toss the pasta with the garlic, anchovies and breadcrumbs. Add lemon juice to taste, toss and serve.

Peas with Leeks
SERVES 12-15

This is a great dish for lots of people as it is so quick to put together.

¼ c olive oil
3 leeks, finely sliced
6-8 slices bacon, finely
chopped

2 lb green peas (can be frozen)
1 c vegetable (or chicken) stock
Salt and freshly ground black pepper

Heat the oil and cook the leeks and bacon over a high heat for 1-2 minutes. Add the peas, stock and seasoning. Bring up to the boil and simmer for 2-3 minutes or until the peas are cooked.

Garlic and Mustard Potatoes

SERVES 12-15 / VEGETARIAN

The flavor of the Dijon mustard goes beautifully with the garlic in this recipe; this is the perfect potato dish for large parties.

2 tbsp butter, softened, plus extra
   for greasing
4 lb potatoes, peeled and sliced
   1/4 in thick
Salt and freshly ground black pepper
1/2 tsp grated nutmeg

3-4 large garlic cloves, peeled
   and chopped
2 1/4 c heavy cream
3 tbsp Dijon mustard
3 oz Parmesan cheese,
   finely grated

Preheat the oven to 350°F (180°C). Using about 1 teaspoon of butter, butter an ovenproof gratin dish about 10 inches square.

Divide the sliced potatoes into three piles. Place one-third of the potatoes on the base of the dish, season with a pinch of salt, pepper, nutmeg and half the chopped garlic, and dot with butter. Then add another layer of potatoes, season the same way, add the remaining garlic, then add a third layer of potatoes and season again.

Heat the cream in a saucepan, stir in the mustard, and pour over the potatoes; it should come just over halfway up the sides of the dish. Scatter with the finely grated Parmesan, cover with foil and place in the oven for 1 1/4-1 1/2 hours. Remove the foil after 30 minutes. The potatoes should be soft and the top should be golden, with the cream bubbling up the sides of the dish.

RACHEL'S HANDY TIP
If this needs to sit and keep warm in the oven for 30 minutes or so, cover it to prevent it drying out.

Rhubarb, Plum and Cardamom Crumble

SERVES 8–10 / VEGETARIAN

Another lovely recipe from my friend Iona Murray. This rich, sweet and perfumed crumble is perfect for entertaining as it can be made in advance. It's also great for large parties as all you have to do is multiply the quantities by two or three.

FOR THE FILLING:

4 tbsp (1/2 stick) butter

1/2 c (4 oz) light brown sugar

14 oz rhubarb, washed and sliced into 1/2-in pieces

8–12 dark red plums, washed, quartered, and pitted

1 tbsp honey

6–8 cardamom pods, pods discarded and seeds crushed

1 cinnamon stick, broken in half

1 strip of lemon peel (using a potato peeler, peel one strip of the lemon zest from top to bottom)

FOR THE TOPPING:

2 1/2 c (11 oz) all-purpose flour

6 tbsp (3 oz) light brown sugar

2 tsp ground cinnamon

14 tbsp (1 3/4 sticks) butter, melted

Approx 1 tbsp granulated sugar, for scattering on top

Preheat the oven to 350°F (180°C). Melt the butter for the filling in a saucepan and stir in the brown sugar. Then add the rhubarb and plums and a tablespoon of water. Mix, add the honey, cardamom seeds, cinnamon and lemon peel, and cook for about 5 minutes, stirring regularly but gently.

Meanwhile, make the topping. Mix together the dry ingredients and add the melted butter, mixing quickly but lightly to form a crumbly texture. Set aside.

Remove the broken cinnamon stick and lemon peel from the fruit mixture and discard. Pour the mixture into a baking dish, then lightly scatter the crumble mixture on top. Do not press down or it will sink and form a mush. Scatter a tablespoon of sugar on top. Cook in the oven for 20–25 minutes or until the top is golden brown and the juices are bubbling up the side. Serve with softly whipped cream or vanilla ice cream.

VARIATION

The topping mixture is also delicious with a good handful of chopped toasted walnuts, hazelnuts or toasted almonds added.

Toffee, Apple and Almond Crumble

SERVES 12 / VEGETARIAN

This has to be one of my favorite desserts—it's completely divine. The toffee sauce keeps for months in the fridge—so handy for a quick sweet treat. It's great with ice cream and baked bananas too. I usually double this recipe, so that I have some left over to store in the fridge.

FOR THE TOFFEE SAUCE:
3/4 c corn syrup
1 c plus 2 tbsp (9 oz) light brown sugar
8 tbsp (1 stick) butter
3/4 c light cream
2 tsp vanilla extract

FOR THE CRUMBLE:
2 3/4 c (12 oz) self-rising flour
Finely grated zest of 2 lemons
10 tbsp butter, chopped or cubed

3/4 c (6 oz) light brown sugar
4 oz ground almonds

FOR THE FILLING:
12 eating apples, peeled, quartered, cored and cut into 3/4-in chunks
4 tbsp butter

TO SERVE:
Softly whipped cream, vanilla ice cream or Crème Anglaise (see page 221)

Preheat the oven to 350°F (180°C). Put all the ingredients for the toffee sauce into a saucepan over a medium heat and boil for 2–3 minutes, stirring regularly until smooth. Set aside.

Next, make the crumble topping. Place the flour and lemon zest in a bowl and rub in the butter, leaving it a little rough and uneven. Stir in the sugar and ground almonds. Place the crumble in the fridge until you are ready to use it.

Melt the 4 tablespoons butter in a wide saucepan or frying pan, add the chopped apples and toss on the heat for a few minutes until the apples start to soften. Add 1/2 cup of the toffee sauce (about half; keep the rest for serving) and continue to simmer for a few minutes longer, until the apples are just cooked.

Pour into two 9-inch pie dishes. Sprinkle the crumble over the top and place in the preheated oven for 20–30 minutes, or until the crumble is light golden and the toffee sauce juices bubble up the sides. Serve warm with softly whipped cream and a jug of the remaining warm toffee sauce.

Lemon and Ginger Ice Cream

SERVES 12 / VEGETARIAN

This is such a delicious, light, one-step ice cream—and you don't need an ice cream machine to make it. Leave out the ginger if you prefer.

1 recipe Lemon Curd, cooled
  (see page 186)
2½ c plain yogurt

2½ c crème fraîche
¼ c finely grated ginger

Fold together the lemon curd, yogurt, crème fraîche and ginger and place in the freezer for a few hours until frozen.

VARIATION

LEMON AND GINGER PUDDING

This is a very quick and easy pudding to make. Make exactly as above, but do not freeze! Serve with Lemon Cookies (see page 45).

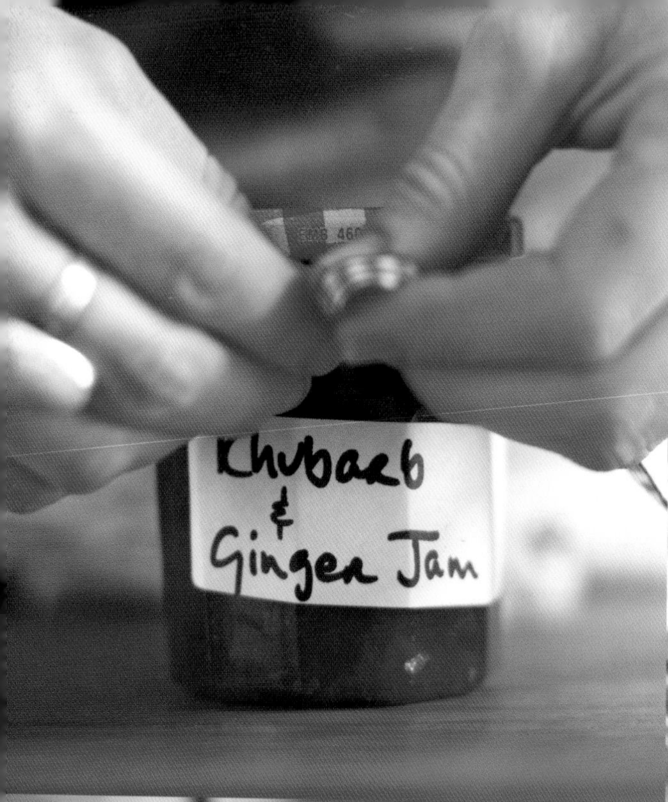

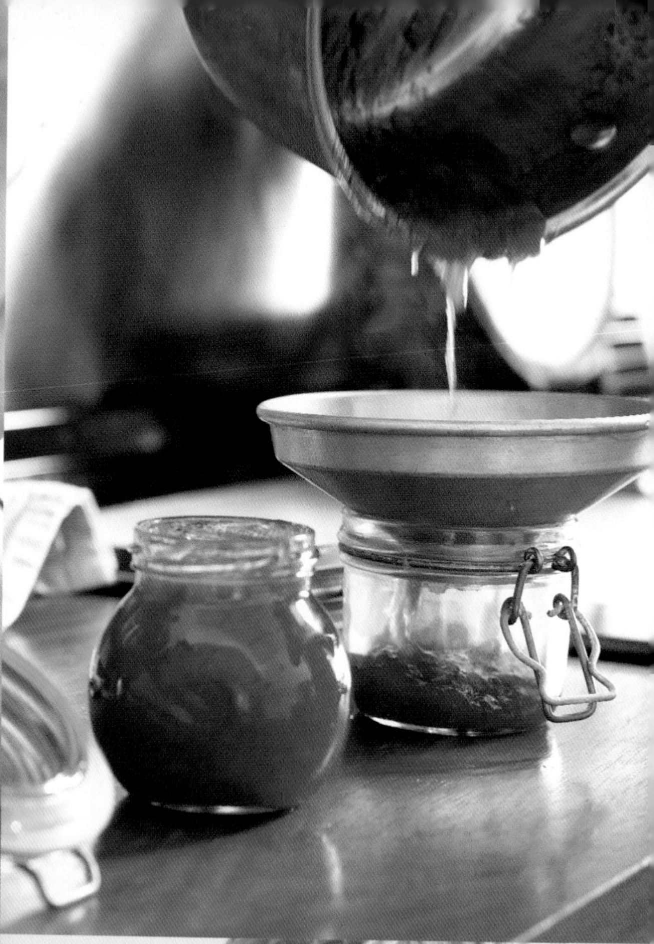

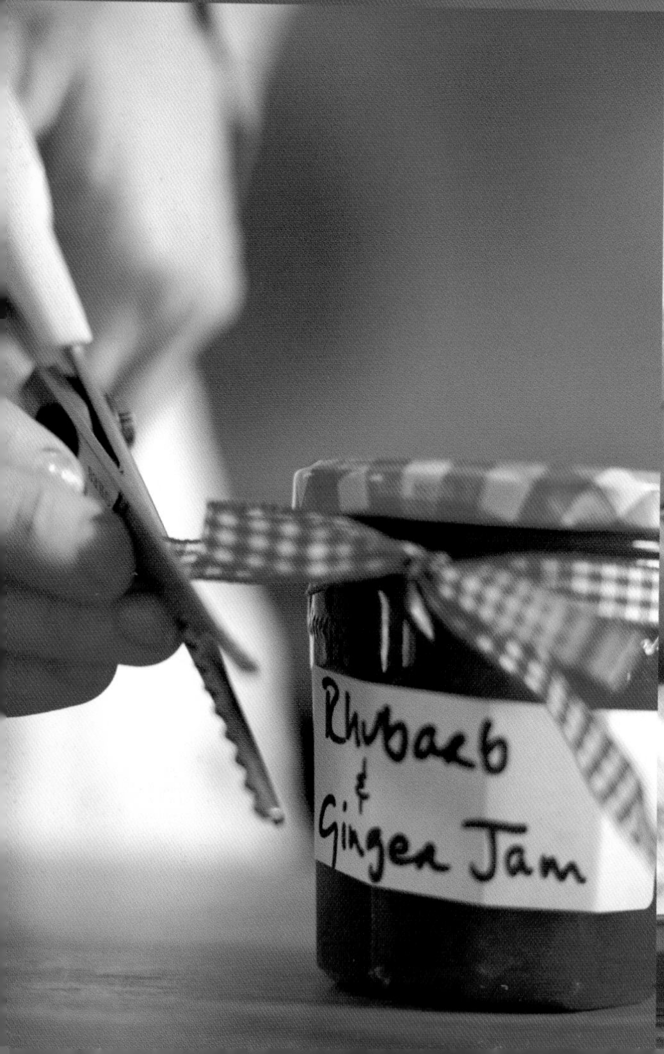

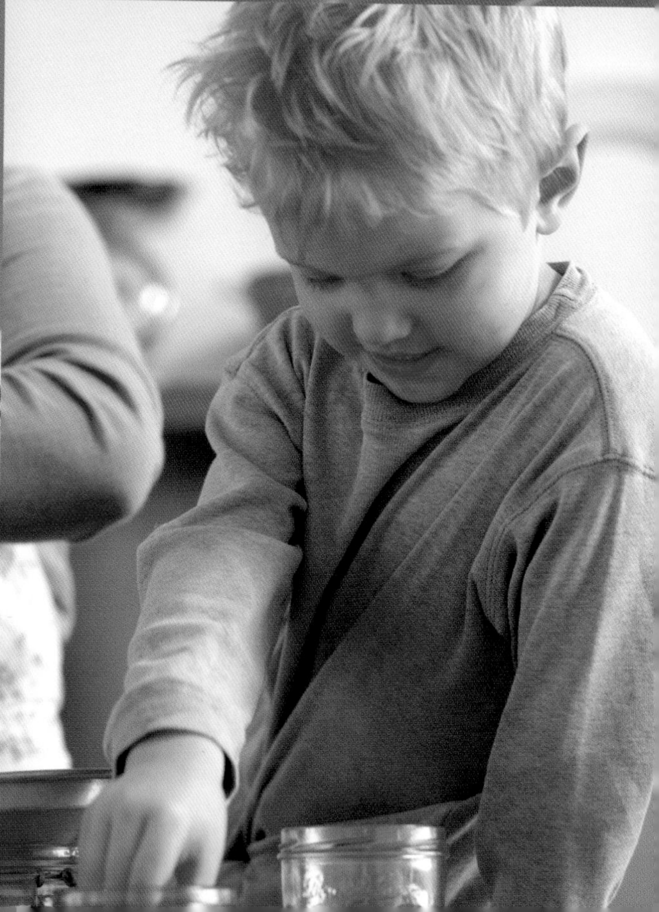

9 Edible Gifts

There is something really lovely about giving and receiving gifts that have been made by hand, and all the better if you can eat them! They're a thoughtful alternative to the usual bottle of wine when going to someone's house for dinner, or as a thank-you present, or a Christmas gift. Jams, chutneys, preserves, cookies, chocolates and fudge can all look so pretty when packaged nicely in lovely jars or bags tied up with ribbon. It's a friendly finishing touch to make your own labels, too— you can be as creative as you wish, and always be sure to include how best to store your gift, and how long it should keep.

Cucumber Pickle

MAKES ABOUT FOUR 1-PINT JARS / VEGETARIAN

Mrs. Allen started making this at Ballymaloe over 30 years ago and it is one of the handiest recipes to have in your repertoire. Not only is it good for burgers and all kinds of sandwiches, but it is wonderful with cold sliced meats and smoked fish, and it transforms a humble hard-boiled egg and a chunk of Cheddar into a meal. It is a true pickle, so even though it will lose its vibrant green color, it will keep for weeks and weeks and weeks. . . .

2 lb unpeeled cucumbers, thinly sliced
3 small onions, peeled and thinly sliced (optional)
1½ c (12 oz) sugar
1 tbsp salt
1 c cider vinegar or white wine vinegar

Mix the cucumber and onion in a large bowl, add the sugar, salt and vinegar, and mix well to combine.

Make 1 hour ahead, if possible, and store in a jar or bowl in the fridge.

Preserved Roasted Peppers with Basil

MAKES 1 MEDIUM-SIZED JAR / VEGETARIAN

I adore having some good roast peppers in the fridge, ready to eat as part of a salad or a Market Plate (see page 214), to throw on top of some freshly cooked pasta or in a sandwich, or whatever takes your fancy! These make a lovely gift potted into a pretty jar and topped up with olive oil.

4 peppers of various colors, left whole
Olive oil
Basil leaves

Preheat the oven to 450°F (230°C). Rub some olive oil over the peppers, then set on a baking sheet in the oven. Cook for about 40 minutes, or until very soft and a little blackened. Take them out of the oven, put into a bowl, cover with plastic wrap and leave to cool.

Once the peppers are cool enough to handle, take them out of the bowl and use your fingers to peel off the skin and break the peppers into quarters. Do not rinse in water or you'll lose the flavor. Then, using a butter knife, scrape the seeds away, which should leave just the flesh. Layer in a sterilized jar (see below), adding basil leaves between the peppers, and fill up with olive oil.

RACHEL'S HANDY TIP
To sterilize jars, either put them through a cycle in your dishwasher, boil them for 5 minutes in a pan of water or place in an oven preheated to 300°F (150°C) for 10 minutes.

Tomato, Ginger and Chile Jam

MAKES TWO 1-PINT JARS / VEGETARIAN

This is a gorgeous, sweet preserve and makes a great gift. It's really versatile—you can enjoy it with everything from cheese and sausages to roast chicken and cold meats.

2 oz ginger, peeled and chopped
4 large garlic cloves, peeled
4 red chiles
2 tbsp fish sauce (nam pla)
1½ lb tomatoes or cherry tomatoes, peeled (see below) and chopped
1¾ c (14 oz) sugar
⅔ c red wine vinegar

Put the ginger, garlic, chiles and fish sauce into a blender and whiz to purée. Place the purée in a saucepan with the tomatoes, sugar and vinegar and bring to the boil. Stir and simmer, uncovered, for about 40 minutes, stirring regularly until thick and jammy. Pour into sterilized jars (see page 177), cover, and allow to cool.

RACHEL'S HANDY TIP

To peel tomatoes, cut a cross in the skin at the base of the tomato and cover with boiling water for 30 seconds. Remove carefully from the hot water and, holding the tomato in a clean tea towel, slip the skins off. If the skins do not come away easily, return to the hot water for another 30 seconds or so.

Spicy Tomato and Apple Chutney

MAKES ABOUT FOUR 1-PINT JARS / VEGETARIAN

A beautiful little jar of this chutney makes a perfect gift. If possible, it is best left to mature for 1–2 weeks before eating.

2¹/₄ lb ripe tomatoes, peeled (see page 178) and chopped
2 onions, peeled and chopped
4 oz golden or regular raisins
1 large cooking apple, peeled, cored and roughly chopped
1¹/₃ c (11 oz) sugar
1 c white wine vinegar
2 tsp salt
¹/₂ tsp allspice
¹/₂ tsp ground ginger
¹/₂ tsp freshly ground black pepper
¹/₂ tsp cayenne pepper

Place all the ingredients in a stainless-steel saucepan and bring up to the boil, stirring. Continue to simmer over a low heat, uncovered, stirring regularly to make sure the bottom does not burn, for about 1 hour or until it is thick and pulpy. Pour into sterilized jars (see page 177) and cover while the chutney is still hot.

Spiced Cranberry and Orange Relish

MAKES ABOUT TWO 1-PINT JARS / VEGETARIAN

A perfect Christmas gift! It will keep for weeks and weeks in a sterilized jar.

12 oz cranberries, fresh or frozen
1 large pinch of ground cinnamon
1 large pinch of ground ginger
Finely grated zest and juice of 1 large orange
3/4 c (6 oz) light muscovado sugar

Place the cranberries (no need to defrost if they are frozen), cinnamon, ginger and the orange juice in a small saucepan and cook over a low heat, with the lid on, stirring often, for about 6–7 minutes, until the cranberries have burst. Take off the heat and stir in the grated orange zest and the sugar. Pour into sterilized jars (see page 177).

Onion Marmalade

MAKES TWO OR THREE 1-PINT JARS / VEGETARIAN

This is a great preserve to give as a gift since it's so versatile. It goes beautifully with cheese, pâtés and cold meats and is perfect with lamb chops or in a steak sandwich. The marmalade keeps well in a sterilized jar for months.

2 tbsp butter
1$\frac{1}{2}$ lb onions, peeled and thinly sliced
$\frac{2}{3}$ c (5 oz) superfine sugar
1 tsp salt
1 tsp freshly ground black pepper
6 tbsp sherry vinegar or balsamic vinegar
1 c full-bodied red wine (it doesn't matter if it has been sitting around for a few days)
2 tbsp crème de cassis (a blackcurrant liqueur)

Melt the butter in a large saucepan and add the onions, sugar, salt and freshly ground pepper. Stir, then cover the saucepan and cook for 30 minutes over a gentle heat, stirring from time to time to prevent the onions from sticking to the bottom of the pan.

Remove the lid and add the vinegar, wine and crème de cassis and cook, uncovered, for another 30 minutes, stirring every now and then. The mixture should be slightly thick by now. Pour into sterilized jars (see page 177) and cover while hot. It will thicken as it cools.

Summer Fruit Jam

MAKES TWO 1-PINT JARS / VEGETARIAN

People always think you are a genius if you make jam, but it really couldn't be easier. So, impress your friends with jammy gifts! If you are going to double this recipe, make sure you use a suitably large saucepan.

1 3/4 c (14 oz) sugar
1 3/4 c (14 oz) summer fruit—a mixture of strawberries, raspberries, red currants, black currants, blackberries and blueberries (you can use frozen fruits out of season)
Juice of 1 lemon

Place the sugar in a heatproof bowl and pop in a moderate oven for 10 minutes to heat up. You can also place the jars in the oven to warm, to prevent them from cracking when the hot jam is poured into them.

Put a saucer in the freezer for testing the jam later on.

Place the fruit (which can be frozen) in a saucepan with the lemon juice and heat up. Simmer for 3 minutes and crush most of the fruit with a potato masher. Add the warm sugar, stir to dissolve and bring up to the boil. Boil for 3–4 minutes over a high heat, stirring regularly.

To test to see if the jam is cooked, take a spoonful of the jam, place it on the frozen plate and allow it to sit for a few seconds. Then push your finger through the blob of jam—if the skin on top forms a wrinkle when pushed, it is cooked. Remove from the heat immediately and pour into sterilized jars (see page 177) or a bowl. A jam funnel is handy for this if you have one. Place the lids on top. The jam will set as it cools.

Orange, Lemon and Grapefruit Marmalade

MAKES ABOUT 5¹/₂ LB OR FIVE OR SIX 1-PINT JARS / VEGETARIAN

There are certain mornings when all I feel like having for breakfast is a nice cup of tea and toast with really good marmalade. This particular recipe is made in the same no-fuss way that my grandpa makes his.

2 oranges
2 grapefruit
2 lemons
Water to cover the fruit plus 4¹/₂ c
5 c (2¹/₂ lb) sugar

Place all the fruit in a large saucepan, cover with water and boil for 1 hour until soft. The lemons may cook slightly faster, so check after 45 minutes and, if soft, remove them while the other fruit finishes cooking.

Take the pan off the heat, discard the cooking water and allow the fruit to cool for a few minutes. Cut the fruit into quarters, then use a spoon to scrape out the pulp, discarding the seeds. Place the pulp in a food processor or blender. If you don't want peel in your marmalade, add the peel to the blender, too. Add ¹/₄ cup of the water and whiz until fine, then push through a sieve into a large saucepan. Add the remainder of the water. If you do want peel in your marmalade, cut the peel into fine slices (or more roughly if you want chunky marmalade) and add to the saucepan.

Bring up to the boil and boil rapidly, uncovered, for 10 minutes, stirring every now and then. Add the sugar, stir until it dissolves, then boil over a high heat for 10 minutes.

Meanwhile, place a saucer in the fridge or freezer. When the marmalade has boiled for 10 minutes, place a blob of the marmalade on the chilled plate and then chill for 1 minute. Push your finger through the blob—if the skin on top forms a wrinkle when pushed, it is cooked. If it is not ready, continue boiling it until it is cooked—this may take up to another 10 minutes, depending on the pectin levels in the fruit. When it is cooked, remove from the heat and pour into sterilized jars (see page 177).

Rhubarb and Ginger Jam

MAKES THREE OR FOUR 1-PINT JARS / VEGETARIAN

I adore this jam—the subtle flavor of the ginger is great with the rhubarb, and it is very quick and easy to make.

2 lb rhubarb, trimmed and sliced
4 c (2 lb) sugar
6 tbsp water
3 tbsp finely grated ginger
1/3 c lemon juice (juice of 2 large or 3 small lemons)

Place a saucer in the freezer. Place all the ingredients in a large saucepan over a medium heat and stir until the sugar dissolves. Turn up the heat, bring to the boil and boil rapidly for 15 minutes until cooked. To test to see if the jam is cooked, take the saucer from the freezer and pour a teaspoon of jam onto it. If a wrinkle forms on the top when you push your finger through the blob, the jam is cooked. Pour into sterilized jars (see page 177) and cover while still hot.

Lemon Curd

MAKES ONE 1-PINT JAR / VEGETARIAN

My aunt, Gay, gave me a lovely big jar full of the most delicious lemon curd for Christmas. It kept me going for weeks—spreading it on toast and drop scones, enjoying it with meringues and cream, and then finally making it into Lemon and Ginger Ice Cream (see page 171). Delicious!

2 eggs
1 egg yolk
8 tbsp (1 stick) butter
3/4 c (6 oz) superfine sugar
Finely grated zest and juice of 3 lemons

Beat the whole eggs and extra egg yolk together. Melt the butter in a saucepan over a very low heat. Add the sugar, grated zest and lemon juice and then the beaten eggs. Stir carefully over a very gentle heat until the mixture thickens. This may take about 10 minutes. If the heat is too high, the eggs will scramble.

When the mixture is thick enough to coat the back of a spoon and leave a clear mark when you push your finger through it, the curd is ready.

Remove from the heat and pour into a sterilized jar (see page 177). Allow to cool, then place in the fridge for up to 2 weeks.

Dark Chocolate and Stem Ginger Cookies

MAKES ABOUT 25 COOKIES / VEGETARIAN

These are gorgeous, intensely flavored little shortbread cookies. Serve them with coffee or pop them into a bag and tie it up with a ribbon for a perfect present.

1¼ c (5 oz) all-purpose flour
¼ c (1 oz) rice flour (if you do not have rice flour, use 1½ c [6 oz] all-purpose flour, although the rice flour gives a lovely crumbly texture)
9 tbsp (1 stick plus 1 tbsp) butter, softened
¼ c (2 oz) light brown sugar
3 oz crystallized ginger, finely chopped
3 oz dark chocolate, chopped

Preheat the oven to 350°F (180°C). Place the flours, butter, sugar, and ginger in a food processor and whiz to combine. If you do not have a food processor, cream the butter and add in the other ingredients, mixing with a wooden spoon until they form a dough.

Roll the dough into balls the size of large cherry tomatoes and place on a baking sheet (no need to grease or line). Using a wet fork, flatten each one slightly and cook in the preheated oven for 8–12 minutes, or until golden and firm. Remove carefully from the pan and cool on a wire rack.

Melt the chocolate gently in a warm oven, a microwave or in a bowl sitting over a saucepan of simmering water. Allow to cool slightly, then use a pastry brush or a butter knife to spread the cookies with the melted chocolate or dip the top of the cookies into the melted chocolate and allow the chocolate to cool and set.

Chocolate Praline Truffles

MAKES ABOUT 40 / VEGETARIAN

These are rich and delicious after-dinner truffles that are well worth the effort of making. They are an impressive gift—who wouldn't love them? For these you need to make praline in which to roll the truffles, but you could always roll them in cocoa powder too. Praline is a lovely, indulgent staple to have on hand in the kitchen. Try sprinkling on top of the Toffee Sundae on page 31.

FOR THE PRALINE:
½ c (4 oz) superfine sugar
4 oz whole almonds
FOR THE TRUFFLES:
2/3 c light cream
8 oz dark chocolate, chopped
1 tbsp whiskey or rum (optional)

First, make the praline. Put a sheet of parchment paper on a baking sheet. Place the sugar and almonds in a saucepan or a nonstick frying pan over a medium heat. Allow the sugar to caramelize slowly; do not stir the mixture, but you can swirl the pan if it is browning unevenly. Cook until all the sugar has caramelized to a rich golden brown (the color of whiskey). Pour the mixture onto the parchment paper and allow to cool completely; it will harden as it cools.

When it is cool, whiz it up in a food processor or place in a plastic bag and bash it with a rolling pin—you want it to become the texture of breadcrumbs. Store in a covered box or jar until you need it; it will keep for a month like this.

To make the truffles, place the cream in a saucepan and bring up to the boil. Then turn off the heat and add the chocolate and the whiskey or rum, if using. Stir until the chocolate has melted and the mixture is smooth. Pour into a shallow pie dish and allow to cool and set. Then either roll into balls with wet hands (nice messy work!) or scoop up with a melon baller or teaspoon (keep dipping it into hot water for easier scooping). Drop into a bowl of praline and toss to cover the chocolates in the crunchy nutty coating. Serve with coffee after dinner.

Heavenly Fudge

MAKES ABOUT 60 PIECES / VEGETARIAN

I adore this fudge—it's sweet, a little bit crumbly and creamy, and oh-so-hard to resist. It takes only 20 minutes to make from start to finish. My sister, Simone, and I used to make fudge with Mum when we were little, and I still make it now.

One 14-oz can sweetened condensed milk
8 tbsp (1 stick) butter
2 c (1 lb) superfine or muscovado sugar

Place the condensed milk, butter and sugar in a saucepan. Stir and bring to the boil. Boil for about 10 minutes, stirring all the time (do not let it burn on the bottom) until it reaches the soft ball stage. To test for this, put a $1/2$ teaspoon blob of the fudge into a bowl of cold water—it should be firm but malleable.

Remove from the heat and set the saucepan in a bowl of cold water that comes $3/4$–$1 1/4$ inches up the outside of the pan. Stir until the fudge cools down a bit— it will go from smooth, shiny and toffeeish to looking thick and grainy.

Scrape the contents of the saucepan into an 8-inch square baking dish or pan with a similar area. The fudge should be $1/2$–$3/4$ inch thick. Let it cool, then cut into squares.

VARIATIONS

VANILLA FUDGE

Add 1 teaspoon of vanilla extract to the ingredients at the start.

CHOCOLATE FUDGE

Add 3 oz dark chocolate (with 70% cocoa solids if possible), chopped, to the fudge when you take it off the heat. Stir to melt the chocolate before placing in the bowl of cold water.

Sinful Butterscotch

My dentist would not approve of this, but I secretly love it! I'd be happy to receive this as a gift any time . . . .

13/4 c (14 oz) sugar
3/4 c plus 2 tbsp water
4 oz powdered glucose (available on the Internet at
www.theindianfoodstore.com)
8 tbsp (1 stick) butter
1/2 tsp salt

Line an 8-inch square pan with wax paper.

Combine the sugar, water and glucose in a saucepan. Stir over a low heat until the sugar is dissolved, bring to the boil and boil for about 15 minutes or until the mixture is light golden brown. Remove from the heat, immediately add the butter and salt, and stir until well blended. Pour into the prepared pan. Mark into squares while still hot. The butterscotch will harden as it cools. Break into pieces.

Vanilla Melting Moments

MAKES 20 / VEGETARIAN

These light, crumbly little cookies literally do melt in your mouth and are absolutely divine.

FOR THE COOKIES:
1¹/₂ c (6 oz) self-rising flour
1 c plus 2 tbsp (4¹/₂ oz) cornstarch
¹/₄ c (2 oz) confectioners' sugar
16 tbsp (2 sticks) butter, cut into pieces
1 tsp vanilla extract

FOR THE VANILLA BUTTER ICING:
4 tbsp (¹/₂ stick) butter, softened
¹/₂ c plus 2 tbsp (4¹/₂ oz) confectioners'
    sugar, plus extra to dust
¹/₂ tsp vanilla extract

Preheat the oven to 325°F (160°C). Place the self-rising flour, cornstarch and confectioners' sugar in a food processor and whiz for a second. Add the butter and vanilla and mix until the dough comes together. Roll the mixture into small balls the size of a large marble, and place on a baking sheet (no need to line) with a little space in between them. Dip a fork in cold water and press down on each one to flatten slightly and score.

Bake for 10–15 minutes until still very pale in color but slightly firm. Remove carefully from the pan and allow to cool on a wire rack.

Meanwhile, make the butter icing. (I usually make this in the food processor bowl in which I have just mixed the cookie dough.) Mix all the ingredients until they come together. Keep at room temperature to remain soft.

When the cookies have cooled, place a butter knife in a cup of boiling water and use the warm, damp knife to spread the icing on one half (take care not to break the cookies). Sandwich with another half. Dust with confectioners' sugar.

RACHEL'S HANDY TIP
If you do not have a food processor, just rub the butter and vanilla into the dry ingredients in a bowl, then work with your hands until the dough comes together.

VARIATION
Make single cookies and brush with approximately 3 oz melted chocolate. Top with small pieces of chopped crystallized ginger.

10 Just Like Mum Used to Make

There are times when we all need something really comforting to eat; food that is warming, wholesome, old-fashioned and hearty, with a hint of nostalgia. Chunky soups, gooey cheese fondue, great bangers and mash, Mum's macaroni and cheese, and a butterscotch pudding will all help to beat the blues on a cold winter's day. This kind of food should be fairly easy and straightforward to make, and will even transport well to the sofa for those times when all you want to do is curl up under a blanket.

Homemade Pork Sausages with Colcannon and Applesauce

SERVES 4 (MAKES ABOUT 12)

For me there is nothing quite so comforting as bangers and mash—sausages and mashed potatoes—and these homemade sausages are ever so tasty and easy to make. They have no casing so are made in a flash, and are great for children and adults alike. Colcannon, which is a traditional Halloween-time Irish mashed potato with cabbage, is perfect winter food. I also love to serve this colcannon with Pork Chops with Caramelized Apples (see page 202).

FOR THE SAUSAGES:
1 lb fatty ground pork
2 oz fresh breadcrumbs
1 egg, whisked
1 garlic clove, peeled and crushed
1 tbsp chopped fresh parsley
  or marjoram
Salt and freshly ground black pepper
3 tbsp olive or sunflower oil

FOR THE COLCANNON:
3 lb floury potatoes, scrubbed
8 tbsp (1 stick) butter
1 lb green cabbage, outer leaves
  removed
2 tbsp water
1 c hot milk
2 tbsp chopped fresh parsley

FOR THE APPLESAUCE:
1 large cooking apple (12 oz), peeled,
  cored and roughly chopped
1 tbsp water
2-4 tbsp (1-2 oz) superfine sugar

For the sausages, mix together all the ingredients except the olive oil, and season with salt and pepper. Fry a tiny bit of the mixture in a pan with a little olive or sunflower oil to see if the seasoning is good.

Divide the mixture into 12 pieces and shape each one into a sausage. Place on a baking sheet or plate and set aside until you want to cook them. (Chilling them for a day in the fridge is fine, or you can freeze them.)

To make the colcannon, cook the potatoes in boiling salted water until tender, draining three-quarters of the water after 5-10 minutes and continuing to cook over a low heat. Avoid stabbing the potatoes with a knife as this will make them break up. When cooked, drain all the remaining water, peel and mash with

4 tablespoons of the butter while hot. I usually hold the potato on a fork and peel with a knife if it is hot.

Meanwhile, cook the cabbage. Cut the cabbage into quarters, then cut out the core. Slice the cabbage finely across the grain. Heat a saucepan, add 2 tablespoons of the butter, the water and the sliced cabbage. Toss over a medium heat for 5–7 minutes, until just cooked. Add to the potatoes, then add the hot milk and the parsley, keeping some of the milk back in case you do not need it all. Season to taste and beat until creamy and smooth, adding more milk if necessary. Serve piping hot with the remaining butter melting in the center.

To make the applesauce, place the apple in a small saucepan with the water. Put the lid on and cook over a gentle heat (stir every now and then) until the apple has broken down to a mush. Add sugar to taste. Serve warm or at room temperature.

To cook the sausages, heat a frying pan on a low to medium heat, add 2 tablespoons of olive or sunflower oil and gently fry the sausages for 12–15 minutes, until golden on all sides and cooked on the inside. Serve with the colcannon and applesauce.

RACHEL'S HANDY TIP
To make breadcrumbs, just put a slice of slightly stale bread (with or without crusts) in a food processor or blender and whiz.

VARIATIONS
The sausage mixture is also delicious shaped into little balls and used instead of the ground beef for Meatballs with Fresh Tomato Sauce (see page 82).

SPICY SAUSAGES WITH CILANTRO
Replace the herbs with 2 tablespoons chopped cilantro, and add half a deseeded, chopped red chile or a pinch of dried chile flakes and serve with sweet chili sauce or Tomato, Ginger and Chile Jam (see page 178).

Baked Eggs and Soldiers

SERVES 6 / VEGETARIAN

These always remind me of when I was little, as we would often have them for an easy brunch or for a late supper.

6 eggs
6 tbsp light cream
1 tbsp butter, divided into 6 knobs
Salt and freshly ground black pepper
Bread, for toasting

Preheat the oven to 325°F (160°C). Bring the kettle to the boil. Break each of the eggs into a ramekin dish, add 1 tablespoon of cream to each and then top with a knob of butter and a pinch of salt and pepper. Place the ramekins in a roasting pan, pour boiling water into the tray so that it comes about halfway up the sides of the dishes and place carefully in the preheated oven. Bake the eggs for 10 minutes or until the eggs are almost set.

Toast some bread until golden, butter it and cut into soldiers (fingers). Serve the baked eggs with hot buttered soldiers on the side.

RACHEL'S HANDY TIP
Try dipping cooked asparagus spears (see page 98) into baked eggs for a sophisticated supper treat.

Chunky Mediterranean Pasta Soup

SERVES 6

This is a gorgeously gutsy soup—definitely a meal in itself. It's the best thing (apart from a sunny beach holiday) for beating the winter blues!

2 tbsp olive oil
1/2 lb chorizo, chopped into
   1/2-in chunks
1 large onion, peeled and chopped
4 large garlic cloves, peeled and
   crushed
Salt and freshly ground black pepper
Two 14 1/2-oz cans chopped tomatoes
   or 2 lb fresh tomatoes, peeled
   (see page 178) and chopped
1 quart chicken stock

2 tbsp chopped fresh herbs—I like to
   use a mixture of rosemary, thyme
   and parsley
Pinch of sugar (optional)
1/2 lb dried pasta, such as orzo
   or fusilli
5 oz shredded spinach or whole baby
   spinach leaves

TO SERVE:
Freshly grated Parmesan cheese
Small bowl of Classic Basil Pesto
   (see page 217)

Heat the olive oil in a large saucepan, add the chorizo and cook for 2 minutes. Add the chopped onion and garlic and season, then cover and sweat over a gentle heat for 7–8 minutes, until soft. Add the tomatoes, stock and herbs. Taste and, if necessary, season again with salt, pepper and a good pinch of sugar, and simmer with the lid on for another 10 minutes or until the tomatoes are soft.

Add the pasta and continue to simmer for another 6–10 minutes, stirring regularly or until the pasta is cooked. When you are ready to serve, drop in the spinach and boil for just 1 minute or until the spinach is wilted. Taste for seasoning. To serve, ladle the chunky soup into large warm bowls and sprinkle with some finely grated Parmesan and a drizzle of pesto.

Pork Chops with Caramelized Apples

SERVES 6

I love this combination of flavors: pork and apples—and cooked like this, they make a perfect supper or big lunch.

2-3 small pork chops per person
Olive oil
Salt and freshly ground black pepper

FOR THE CARAMELIZED APPLES:
2 tbsp butter
3 eating apples, peeled, cored and cut into slices $1/4$ in thick
2 tbsp sugar
Juice of $1/2$ lemon

Drizzle the chops with a little olive oil and black pepper. Leave to sit in the fridge until you need to cook them—all day is fine.

Preheat the oven to 375°F (190°C). Place a baking sheet in the oven to heat up.

To prepare the caramelized apples, heat the butter in a frying pan. Add the apples and the sugar and toss on the heat for 4–5 minutes until cooked and golden. Squeeze in the lemon juice and keep warm.

Heat a frying pan until very hot, then cook the chops in batches, on both sides until golden. Sprinkle with salt, then pop them onto the hot baking sheet in the oven and cook for another 5–10 minutes or until cooked through.

Serve the pork chops with the caramelized apples and some Garlic and Mustard Potatoes (see page 167) on the side.

Steak with Blue Cheese Butter and Walnut Salad

SERVES 2

This is serious comfort food and takes only 5 minutes to prepare, which is perfect for those times when you have just come home from work and need some real food fast!

FOR THE STEAKS:
2 sirloin or ribeye steaks, approx 6-8 oz each, excess fat removed
A drizzle of olive oil
Sea salt and freshly ground black pepper

FOR THE BLUE CHEESE BUTTER:
1 oz blue cheese, rind removed
2 tbsp butter
Freshly ground black pepper

FOR THE SALAD:
2 handfuls of a mixture of watercress, arugula and baby spinach
A drizzle of olive oil (about 1 tbsp)
A small squeeze of lemon juice (about 1/2-1 tsp)
Sea salt and freshly ground black pepper
2 tbsp chopped walnuts, tossed over the heat in a dry pan until golden

Place the pan for the steaks on the heat. Drizzle the steaks with olive oil and sprinkle with black pepper, then allow to sit while the pan heats up.

To make the blue cheese butter, mash together the blue cheese and the butter in a bowl. Add some black pepper, then form into a log and wrap in plastic. Pop in the fridge to cool, or the freezer if you have just a few minutes.

When the pan is very hot, sprinkle the steaks with sea salt and place in the pan. Cook until one side turns a deep golden color and is seared, then turn over and cook until they are how you like them, 1–2 minutes for rare, about 4 minutes for medium or 8-10 minutes on a lower heat (so they don't burn) for well done. The cooking times will vary depending on the thickness of the steaks and the heat of the pan. When the steaks are cooked, take them off the heat and allow to rest while you toss the salad leaves with the olive oil, lemon juice, sea salt and pepper. Put the steaks on warm plates and top with slices of blue cheese butter. Serve with the dressed leaves sprinkled with chopped walnuts.

Macaroni and Cheese

SERVES 6-8 / VEGETARIAN

Macaroni and cheese must be the ultimate cure-all for adults and children alike. You can also add small pieces of cooked ham or bacon to the sauce. Macaroni and cheese can be made in advance and then reheated when you are ready to serve.

6 tbsp (3/4 stick) butter
1 onion, peeled and chopped
3/4 c (3 oz) all-purpose flour
3 3/4 c boiling milk
1-2 tsp Dijon mustard
8 oz cheese (Cheddar, or, even better, half Cheddar and half
   Gruyère), grated
Salt and freshly ground black pepper
11 oz elbow macaroni

Melt the butter in a saucepan, add the chopped onion and cook gently until soft. Stir in the flour and cook for a minute, then gradually add the milk, whisking all the time, and the mustard. Whisk in three-quarters of the cheese and allow to melt into the sauce, then season to taste with salt and pepper.

Cook the pasta in a large pot of boiling water with a teaspoon of salt, until just soft. Drain, then toss into the cheese sauce and transfer to a gratin dish about 10 inches square. Sprinkle with the remaining cheese and pop under a broiler for a few minutes to brown the cheese on top, or if you wish, put this aside for later. To reheat, put the dish in an oven preheated to 400°F (200°C) for about 25 minutes, or until golden and bubbling.

Oven-baked Risotto with Mushrooms and Thyme

SERVES 4-6 / VEGETARIAN

Risotto goes straight to the heart of both children and adults. You can always leave out the mushrooms if you wish.

Scant 1 oz dried mushrooms, such as porcini or a mixture of types
1 3/4 c boiling water
2 tbsp olive oil
1 small onion, peeled and chopped
2 garlic cloves, peeled and crushed
Salt and freshly ground black pepper

12 oz risotto rice, such as carnaroli or arborio
1 tsp thyme leaves, chopped plus 1 tsp whole leaves, for garnish
3 1/4 c hot vegetable (or chicken) stock
1/2 c white wine
3 oz Parmesan cheese, grated

Preheat the oven to 350°F (180°C). Place the dried mushrooms in a bowl, add the boiling water and leave to soak for 10 minutes. Meanwhile, heat the olive oil in a medium ovenproof saucepan or casserole and cook the onion and garlic for a few minutes until soft and a little golden. Season with salt and pepper.

Drain and chop the mushrooms, and reserve the liquid. Add the mushrooms to the garlic and onions with the rice, chopped thyme and the sieved, drained mushroom-soaking liquid. Pour in the stock and wine, bring to the boil and season to taste. Cover with the lid, place in the preheated oven and cook for 15–20 minutes, or until the rice is just cooked and all the liquid has been absorbed. Stir in about two-thirds of the grated Parmesan and check the seasoning. To serve, sprinkle with the remaining Parmesan and thyme leaves.

RACHEL'S HANDY TIP
The alcohol in the wine burns off during the cooking of the risotto and the flavor is lovely, but if you do not want to use it, just replace it with extra stock.

Fondue Savoyard

SERVES 4-6 / VEGETARIAN

There are not many cold-weather suppers (or lunches on the ski slopes) better than this: pieces of bread dipped into molten cheese. You can either invest in a fondue set (fun and handy for large numbers), or you can make a fondue for two in a saucepan on a very low flame on the stovetop and eat it right beside the stove or even a camping stove! You need a good white bread for dipping, and, as with the Raclette (see page 145), charcuterie and gherkins are nice to have on the side, but not essential. Don't forget that if your piece of bread falls off your fork you have to kiss the person to your left, so it is important to position yourself very carefully!

1 garlic clove, peeled and cut in half
1¼ c light dry white wine
1½ lb Gruyère, Beaufort or Raclette cheese, or a mixture of all three, grated

Pinch of grated nutmeg
Freshly ground black pepper
2 tbsp kirsch (optional)
1 loaf of good white or sourdough bread, cut into 3/4-in cubes

Rub the inside of a medium-sized saucepan with the garlic, then discard the garlic. Add the wine to the pan and bring to the boil over a high heat (this will get rid of the alcohol in the wine). Reduce the heat to medium and gradually add the cheese, stirring constantly with a wooden spoon to melt it—do not allow it to boil. Continue to cook for a few more minutes, add the nutmeg, pepper and kirsch and transfer to a fondue pot (if using).

Serve the cubed bread in a basket on the table. Using fondue forks (or just plain forks), dip pieces of bread into the cheese. Keep a wooden spoon in the fondue and stir it every now and then. Place it back on the heat for a few seconds if it cools down too much.

Bill Granger's Banana Butterscotch Pudding

SERVES 4-6 / VEGETARIAN

I absolutely adore this pudding from Bill's book, *Simply Bill*. He made this when I appeared with him on *Great Food Live*, and as soon as I tasted it I was hooked. I have adapted the recipe slightly to fit the pie dish that I have. To make this for 12 people, double this recipe and cook in a 10-inch square gratin dish for 55 minutes.

FOR THE PUDDING:
1 c (4 oz) all-purpose flour
1 tbsp baking powder
½ c (4 oz) superfine sugar
1 egg, beaten
1 banana, mashed
1 c milk
1 tsp vanilla extract
6 tbsp (3/4 stick) butter, melted

FOR THE TOPPING:
½ c (4 oz) light brown sugar
2 tbsp corn syrup
2/3 c boiling water

TO SERVE:
Softly whipped cream or vanilla
  ice cream

Preheat the oven 350°F (180°C). Sift the flour and baking powder into a bowl. Add the sugar. Mix together the beaten egg, the mashed banana, milk, vanilla extract and melted butter. Pour into the dry ingredients and stir to mix until combined. Pour this wet dough into a 9-inch pie dish and place the dish on a baking sheet.

To make the topping, put the brown sugar, corn syrup and boiling water in a saucepan. Bring to the boil and then drizzle it all over the pudding. Bake in the preheated oven for 30–40 minutes, or until it feels slightly firm in the center. Serve with softly whipped cream or vanilla ice cream. If you're not going to serve the pudding immediately, keep it somewhere warm until you are ready—it sits quite happily.

Chocolate Comfort in a Cup

SERVES 2 / VEGETARIAN

Also known as hot chocolate! It always takes me right back to when I was little and on holiday staying with my grandparents in Canada. They always made us hot chocolate with lots of mini marshmallows on top, which slowly melt as you drink it. Heaven!

2 c milk

5 oz milk chocolate

2 tsp cocoa

2 tbsp mini marshmallows

Put the milk, chocolate and cocoa into a saucepan. Stirring all the time, warm over a low heat until the chocolate has melted, the cocoa dissolved and the mixture has almost come to the boil. Take off the heat and pour into two cups. Sprinkle with mini marshmallows and serve.

Vin Chaud

SERVES 4-6 / VEGETARIAN

Each café and restaurant on the slopes in the Alps has its own secret recipe for vin chaud—hot wine with spices. Sipping this at home on a wintry, drizzly night in Ireland makes me dream of skiing holidays.

1 bottle dry, fruity red wine

$1/4$ c crème de cassis or brandy

$1/2$ c (4 oz) superfine sugar

Finely grated zest of $1/2$ lemon and
  $1/2$ orange

Good pinch of grated nutmeg

2 cinnamon sticks

6 whole cardamom pods

6 cloves

Orange slices, to serve

Place all the ingredients except the orange slices in a saucepan and very gently simmer (do not boil) for about 5–10 minutes to let the flavors of the spices infuse. Strain if you like, and serve in warmed glasses, with a slice of orange in each one.

Useful Extras

The recipes in this section are either classic kitchen staples that form the backbone of so many wonderful dishes, or are timeless accompaniments. I use all of them on a regular basis, and many are called for in the recipes throughout this book.

Market Plate

Ironically enough (as it involves hardly any actual cooking), this is one of my favorite meals. We are very fortunate now to have so many excellent farmers' markets close to us, with stallholders selling everything from fabulous local potatoes to the most delicious locally made salamis and cheeses. What a delight it is to be able to go to a market and come back laden down with a basketful of the most amazing food, ready to go straight on the table—now that's what I call convenience food!

Of course, not all markets will have everything I list on this page, nor might you want it all, but this is a guide to inspire more than to tell you what to do. You will know what combinations you want on your table. And you can serve as many or as few of these selections as you like. They make a great meal for a casual dinner party or for a lunch (alfresco or not), and also travel incredibly well to make a delicious picnic.

BREAD: white, whole wheat, baguette, sourdough, foccacia—many farmers' markets sell wonderful artisan breads baked that morning

SELECTION OF CHARCUTERIE: salamis (venison, pork and garlic, chorizo, etc.), cured meats such as Parma and Serrano ham

CHEESE: try your local and imported cheeses, aiming for a good selection, such as a goat cheese, a Brie, a hard cheese, a semi-soft, a blue and a local Cheddar

SMOKED FISH: try smoked salmon, even hot-smoked salmon, or smoked mackerel, eel, mussels or trout

SMOKED MEAT: smoked chicken and duck are really delicious

Buy, or make, some Cucumber Pickle (see page 174)—this is great with smoked fish, charcuterie and cheese. Pick up or make some Mayonnaise (see page 216), also delicious with smoked fish. Make your own or buy some chutneys and relishes, like Tomato, Ginger and Chile Jam (see page 178), Spicy Tomato and Apple Chutney (see page 179) or Onion Marmalade (see page 181). Buy or make Preserved Roasted Peppers with Basil (see page 177), Olive Paste (see page 102) and Classic Basil Pesto (see page 217).

Always have on hand a gorgeous bottle of olive oil to drizzle over your bread (or truffle oil for a special treat), some dolmades (stuffed grape leaves), capers and anchovies.

Roux

VEGETARIAN

Roux is a basic and simple sauce thickener made with equal quantities of butter and flour so if you find yourself using quite a lot, you can easily increase the quantities. It is handy to have in the fridge and it keeps for 2–3 weeks.

8 tbsp (1 stick) butter

1 c (4 oz) all-purpose flour

Heat a saucepan over a medium heat and melt the butter, then add the flour, continuing to stir on the heat. Allow it to cook for 2 minutes. Pour into a bowl and use straight away, or allow to cool and put in the fridge.

Stock

Making stock is incredibly easy—it's just a state of mind! It takes only 5 minutes to throw everything into the pot; let it cook for a while and you are halfway to creating a really wholesome, nutritious soup. Stock keeps in the fridge for 2–3 days and freezes very well. To defrost, reheat in a saucepan.

Chicken carcass, raw or cooked (optional)
1–2 carrots
1 onion or leek

1 celery stalk
1 small bay leaf
1 sprig of parsley
1 sprig of thyme

Put all the ingredients in a large saucepan, fill up the pot with cold water, and bring to the boil. Turn down the heat and let it simmer for 1–2 hours. Season to taste and then strain the stock and discard the bits. Skim the fat off the stock as it cools.

Mayonnaise

MAKES 1¼ CUPS / VEGETARIAN

Homemade mayonnaise is so delicious. It can bring the simplest sandwich or salad to life and is great to have on hand for those last-minute snacks. Keep it covered in the fridge and it will last for at least a week.

2 egg yolks
Salt
1 tsp Dijon mustard

2 tsp white wine vinegar
1 c oil—I like to use 3/4 c sunflower oil
  and ¼ c olive oil

Put the egg yolks into a glass mixing bowl and add a pinch of salt, the mustard and the vinegar. Whisk together. Very gradually, add all the oil drop by drop, whisking all the time (I often use an electric hand blender). When you have whisked in all the oil, it should look thick and creamy. Add a good pinch of salt to taste.

VARIATION

Basic mayonnaise works incredibly well with many other flavors. Try varying your recipe by adding ground spices, chopped herbs or olives, or even chopped sun-dried tomatoes for unique flavors.

Mint Sauce

MAKES ABOUT ¼ CUP / VEGETARIAN

The classic sauce to serve with good old Roast Leg of Lamb (see page 102). It's made in minutes.

3 tbsp chopped fresh mint
2 tbsp superfine or light brown sugar
¼ c boiling water

1 tbsp lemon juice or white wine
  vinegar

Place the mint and sugar in a bowl and add the boiling water. Stir until the sugar is dissolved. Add the lemon juice or vinegar and let it cool for about 10 minutes before serving.

Classic Basil Pesto

MAKES ONE 1-PINT JAR / VEGETARIAN

Serve this versatile pesto with pasta, roasted or chargrilled vegetables, barbecued or grilled meats, as part of a salad, or on a simple crostini or bruschetta with roasted peppers and cheese. Try making variations by replacing the basil with parsley or arugula or wild garlic leaves—the possibilities are endless! It freezes very well, too.

2 oz basil leaves
1 oz Parmesan cheese,
   freshly grated
2 tbsp pine nuts

1 garlic clove, peeled and crushed
1/3 c olive oil
Salt

Put all the ingredients except the olive oil and salt into a food processor and blend. Add the oil and a pinch of salt, blend again and taste. Pour into a sterilized jar (see page 177), cover with a 1/2-inch layer of oil and store in the fridge.

Red Currant Jelly

MAKES TWO 1-PINT JARS / VEGETARIAN

This simple red currant jelly is another fine addition to Roast Leg of Lamb (see page 102).

1 lb fresh or frozen red currants,
   destalked

2 c (1 lb) sugar

Put the currants and sugar in a saucepan on a medium heat and stir until the sugar dissolves and the mixture begins to boil. Turn up the heat and boil rapidly for 6 minutes, stirring occasionally to prevent it sticking. Spoon off any froth that accumulates on top and pour the mixture into a sieve (not aluminum) and allow it to drip through into a bowl. Do not be tempted to push it through or the jelly will become cloudy. If you want to keep this for later use, pour the jelly into clean, sterilized jam jars (see page 177) immediately. After it has cooled and set a little, it will be ready to eat, or you can store it in the fridge. It will keep for months.

Rice

SERVES 6-8 / VEGETARIAN

A big bowl of rice is just what you need to serve with stew or curry, and is so convenient to cook for large numbers of people.

PLAIN BOILED RICE

1 lb white rice, such as Basmati

1 tsp salt

1 tbsp butter (optional)

Preheat the oven to 275°F (140°C). Bring a large saucepan of water to the boil. Add the rice and salt, give it a stir, cover and boil rapidly for 4–5 minutes, or until the rice is nearly cooked but still has a tiny bite. Strain the rice and place in a serving dish. Stir in the butter, if using, cover and put in the oven for at least 15 minutes. If you want to get the rice into the oven 30 minutes before you eat, just preheat it to 200°F (100°C).

When ready to eat, fluff up the rice and serve. Sometimes I add whole spices to the water, such as a small cinnamon stick or two or three star anise and a few green cardamom pods, and serve them on top of of the rice.

PILAF RICE

2 tbsp butter

1 small onion, peeled and chopped

11 oz Basmati rice

3¼ c vegetable (or chicken) stock

Salt and freshly ground black pepper

Melt the butter in a saucepan large enough to contain all the rice. Add the chopped onion, put on the lid and cook over a low heat for about 10 minutes until the onion is soft. Add the rice and stir on the heat for about 2 minutes. Add the stock and some salt and pepper, cover, bring to the boil, then turn the heat right down to minimum and simmer on top of the stove for about 10 minutes until the rice is just cooked and all the liquid absorbed. Alternatively, cook in an oven at 325°F (160°C). Cover and keep warm if you need to.

THAI RICE

14 oz Thai fragrant rice　　　　　　　　**Approximately 13/4 c water**

Place the rice and water in a medium-sized saucepan. There are a few ways of gauging the correct amount of water to put in, as it depends on the size of saucepan used. The method I use is to put my index finger into the water, pointing down, and just touching the rice. The water should come up to the first knuckle.

Bring to the boil, stir once, then cover with a lid (or a heatproof glass plate is quite handy as you can see inside). Turn the heat down to the lowest possible level. Continue to cook for 11–15 minutes, then have a quick look. The rice should be cooked and have absorbed all the liquid. Remove from the heat, keep covered and allow to sit for 5 minutes before serving. The rice will stay warm for a while.

Savory Shortcrust Pastry

MAKES 1LB PASTRY / VEGETARIAN

This makes enough to line one 10- or 11-inch square pan (with a little left over), or two 8-inch round pans (it is best if they have removable bases). Uncooked pastry freezes perfectly, so it is handy to have some in the freezer. It will also keep in the fridge for a couple of days.

2 c (9 oz) all-purpose flour

9 tbsp (1 stick plus 1 tbsp) butter, diced and softened

$^1/_2$–1 egg, beaten

Place the flour and butter in a food processor. Whiz for a few seconds, then add half the beaten egg and continue whizzing. You might need to add a little more egg, but don't add too much—the pastry should just come together. (If making by hand, rub the butter into the flour, then use your hands to bring it together with the egg.) Flatten out the ball of dough to a thickness of about 1$^1/_4$ inches, wrap or cover with plastic, and place in the fridge for at least 30 minutes.

When you are ready to roll the pastry, remove from the fridge. Place the pastry between two sheets of plastic, which should be bigger than your tart pan. Using a rolling pin, roll it out until it is no thicker than $^1/_8$ inch. Make sure to keep it round, if the pan is round, and large enough to line the base and sides of the pan.

Removing the top layer of plastic wrap, place the pastry upside-down (plastic facing up) in the tart pan. Press into the edges, plastic attached and, using your thumb, "cut" the pastry on the edge of the pan to give a neat finish. Remove the plastic and pop the pastry in the freezer for at least 10 minutes.

BLIND BAKING

Blind baking is a way of partially cooking a pastry shell before adding its filling. Preheat the oven to 350°F (180°C). Line the pastry with wax paper when cold (leaving plenty to come up the sides), fill with pie weights or dried beans (you can use these over and over), and bake for 15–20 minutes, until the pastry feels dry. Remove the paper and beans, brush with a little leftover beaten egg and return to the oven for 2 minutes. Take out of the oven and put to one side while you prepare the filling. This can be easily made a day in advance.

SWEET PASTRY
Use the recipe for savory pastry but add 2 tbsp confectioners' sugar to the flour and butter in the food processor at the start of the method.

Sugar Syrup
MAKES 3/4 CUP / VEGETARIAN

This is the basic sugar syrup recipe used for things such as cocktails and poaching fruit. It keeps indefinitely and it is very handy to have some available.

1 c (8 oz) superfine sugar   1 c water

Place the ingredients in a saucepan and bring slowly to the boil, stirring to dissolve the sugar. When the sugar has dissolved, boil for 2 minutes and allow to cool.

Crème Anglaise
MAKES 21/4 CUPS / VEGETARIAN

This is a classic custard sauce that is delicious poured over a crumble or an apple pie.

21/4 c milk   5 egg yolks
1 vanilla pod   1/2 c (4 oz) superfine sugar

Bring the milk to the boil with the vanilla pod. In a large bowl, beat the egg yolks and sugar until pale and thick. Gradually whisk in the hot milk and add the mixture back into the saucepan. Cook over a very low heat, stirring all the time with a wooden spoon until the mixture thickens slightly; it should just coat the back of a spoon. Remove the vanilla pod. Pour into a pitcher and serve warm. If you are reheating this, do so very carefully on a low heat.

Index

almonds: chocolate and almond cake, 49
  chocolate praline truffles, 189
  little almond brittles, 48
  no-pastry pear and almond tart, 32
amaretti cookie ice cream, 111
anchovies, pasta with garlic and, 166
apples: apple and cinnamon muffins, 15
  applesauce, 196-8
  pork chops with caramelized apples, 202
  spicy tomato and apple chutney, 179
  toffee, apple and almond crumble, 170
  upside-down apple and cinnamon cake, 29
apricots: chewy seedy oat and apricot bars, 88
arugula: crispy bacon, tomato and arugula salad, 116-17
  arugula, tomato and sugar snap pea salad, 59
asparagus: asparagus and scallion tart, 61
  asparagus soldiers with boiled eggs, 117
  asparagus with easy hollandaise sauce, 98
avocados: avocado, orange and watercress salad, 123
  crab and avocado salad, 123

bacon: bacon and Parmesan scones, 91
  bacon, tomato and arugula salad, 116-17
  Gruyère cheese and crispy bacon, 138
baking blind, 220
bananas: banana and cinnamon smoothie, 75
  banana and peanut butter muffins, 84
  banana butterscotch pudding, 209
basil pesto, 217
beans see white beans
beef: beef stew with brandy, 104
  beef with prunes and peppers, 160
  classic spaghetti and meatballs, 82-3
  South American beef steak, 127
  spaghetti with olives, capers, anchovies and, 105
  steak with blue cheese butter, 203
  Thai stir-fried beef, 158
berry muffins, 15
bok choy: light coconut broth with, 97
  Thai stir-fried beef with red peppers and, 158
brandy: brandy cream, 49
  little hot after-dinner shots, 112
bread: baked eggs and soldiers, 199
  chest of sandwiches, 56
  creamy tomatoes on toast, 144
  market plate, 214
  muffleta, 54-5
  Parmesan toasts, 19
  toasted ham and Gruyère sandwich, 140
broccoli soup with Parmesan toasts, 19
butternut squash, chorizo and feta frittata, 63

butterscotch, 191
  banana butterscotch pudding, 209

cabbage: colcannon, 196-8
cakes: cardamom sour cream cake, 36
  chocolate and almond cake, 49
  chocolate cake for birthday parties, 38-9
  orange and chocolate chip celebratory cupcake, 42
  porter cake, 41
  sponge cake with rhubarb cream, 50
  upside-down apple and cinnamon cake, 29
  upside-down rhubarb and ginger cake, 28
Campari cocktails, 128
cardamom sour cream cake, 36
casseroles, 104, 153-4, 160
cheese: crispy bacon and Parmesan scones, 91
  fondue Savoyard, 207
  gratin of fish with, 106
  Gruyère cheese and crispy bacon, 138
  macaroni and cheese, 204
  market plate, 214
  muffleta, 54-5
  onion and blue cheese tart, 118
  Parmesan chicken fingers, 79
  Parmesan toasts, 19
  potato, chorizo and feta frittata, 63
  quesadillas, 76
  raclette, 145
  Serrano ham and Manchego cheese, 136
  Sicilian pasta, 165
  steak with blue cheese butter, 203
  toasted ham and Gruyère sandwich, 140
chest of sandwiches, 56
chicken: chicken, ginger and cashew stir-fry, 16
  chicken pie with ham and peas, 100-1
  chicken pilaf, 153
  Parmesan chicken fingers, 79
  quesadillas with, 76
chickpeas: hummus, 139
chiles: scrambled eggs with tomato, chile and cilantro, 12
  tomato, ginger and chile jam, 178
chimichurri sauce, 127
chocolate: chocolate and almond cake, 49
  chocolate cake for birthday parties, 38-9
  chocolate comfort in a cup, 210
  chocolate fudge, 190
  chocolate and hazelnut toffee tart, 109
  chocolate praline truffles, 189
  dark chocolate and stem ginger cookies, 187
  hot mocha sauce, 111
  little almond brittles, 48
  orange and chocolate chip celebratory cupcake, 42

chorizo: potato, chorizo and feta frittata, 63
chutney, spicy tomato and apple, 179
cilantro and lime raita, 143
cocktails, 128
coconut milk: coconut cilantro sauce, 156-7
  light coconut broth with bok choy and basil, 97
coffee: crème brûlée au café, 110-11
  hot mocha sauce, 111
colcannon, 196-8
cookies: dark chocolate and stem ginger cookies, 187
  jam drops, 91
  lemon cookies, 45
  little almond brittles, 48
  vanilla melting moments, 192
  whole wheat shortbread cookies, 46
couscous, lemon and pomegranate, 154
crab: crab and avocado salad, 123
  Vietnamese crab salad, 162
cranberry and orange relish, 180
cream, brandy, 49
crème Anglaise, 221
crème brûlée au café, 110-11
crème fraîche with sweet chili dip, 139
crumbles, 169-70
crumpets, 87
cucumber: cucumber pickle, 174
  tomato and cucumber salsa, 139
custard: crème Anglaise, 221
  crème brûlée au café, 110-11
  custard tart, 131

dips, 83, 139
dressings: honey mustard, 150
  walnut, 136
drop scones, 87
duck, lentil and red cabbage salad, 60

eggs: asparagus soldiers with softly boiled eggs, 117
  baked eggs and soldiers, 199
  ham and egg pie, 64
  potato, chorizo and feta frittata, 63
  scrambled eggs, 12, 72
  summer omelette, 116-17

fish: gratin of fish with cheese, tomatoes and herbs, 106
  Parmesan fish fingers, 80
  See also anchovies, crab, mackerel, salmon, shrimp, tuna
fondue Savoyard, 207
frittata: potato, chorizo and feta, 63
fruit: summer fruit jam, 182
  summer tiramisu, 130
fruit cakes: porter cake, 41
fruity breakfast muffins, 14-15
fudge, 190

garlic: garlic and mustard potatoes, 167
  pasta with garlic and anchovies, 166
  roast leg of lamb with, 102

warm pasta salad with herbs, garlic and
arugula, 124
gin: cool Campari and lime gin and tonic,
128
ginger: dark chocolate and stem ginger
cookies, 187
lemon and ginger ice cream, 171
rhubarb and ginger jam, 185
goat cheese: muffleta, 54–5
gratin of fish, 106
green leaf and pea soup, 120
green salad with honey mustard dressing,
150
Gruyère cheese and crispy bacon, 138

ham: chicken pie with bacon and peas,
100–1
ham and egg pie, 64
Serrano ham and Manchego cheese,
136
toasted ham and Gruyère sandwich,
140
hazelnuts: chocolate and hazelnut toffee
tart, 109
herb scones, 90
hollandaise sauce, 98
honey mustard dressing, 150
hummus, 139

ice cream: amaretti cookie ice cream, 111
lemon and ginger ice cream, 171
toffee sundae, 31

jam drops, 91
jam tarts, 68
jams: rhubarb and ginger, 185
summer fruit, 182

ketchup, tomato, 80

lamb: lamb samosas, 143
Moroccan lamb tagine, 154
roast leg of lamb with garlic, 102
leeks, peas with, 166
lemon: lemon and ginger ice cream, 171
lemon and ginger pudding, 171
lemon cookies, 45
lemon curd, 186
lentils: duck, lentil and red cabbage salad,
60
little almond brittles, 48
little hot after-dinner shots, 112

macaroni and cheese, 204
mackerel, pan-fried with herb butter, 27
maple syrup and pecan muffins, 67
market plate, 214
marmalade: orange, lemon and
grapefruit, 184
mascarpone: summer tiramisu, 130
mayonnaise, 216
meatballs, classic spaghetti and, 82–3
meringue: baked meringue with peaches,
132
milk: chocolate comfort in a cup, 210
mint sauce, 216
mocha sauce, 111
Moroccan lamb tagine, 154

muffins: banana and peanut butter, 84
berry breakfast, 14–15
maple syrup and pecan, 67
muffleta, 54–5
mushrooms: beef stew with brandy, 104
chicken pie with bacon and peas, 100–1
oven-baked risotto with, 206
mustard and honey dip, 83

nectarine, berry and plum smoothie, 75
noodles: chicken, ginger and cashew stir-
fry with coconut noodles, 16
Vietnamese crab salad with rice
noodles, 162

oats: chewy seedy oat and apricot bars, 88
yogurt with oats and honey, 72
omelette with crispy bacon, tomato and
arugula salad, 116–17
onions: muffleta, 54–5
onion and blue cheese tart, 118
onion marmalade, 181
oranges: avocado, orange and watercress
salad, 123
orange and chocolate chip celebratory
cupcake, 42
orange, lemon and grapefruit
marmalade, 184
spiced cranberry and orange relish, 180

Parmesan chicken fingers, 79
Parmesan fish fingers, 80
party sausages, 83
pasta: chunky Mediterranean pasta soup,
200
classic spaghetti and meatballs, 82–3
creamy pasta with sun-dried tomatoes,
olives and pine nuts, 24
macaroni and cheese, 204
pasta with garlic, anchovies and
breadcrumbs, 166
pasta with spinach, bacon and
Parmesan, 23
pasta with tomato and ginger salsa and
crème fraîche, 99
Sicilian pasta, 165
spaghetti with beef, olives, capers and
anchovies, 105
warm pasta salad with herbs, garlic and
arugula, 124
pastry, savory shortcrust, 220
peaches: baked meringue with, 132
peach muffins, 14
peanut butter: banana and peanut butter
muffins, 84
chewy seedy oat and apricot bars, 88
pears: no-pastry pear and almond tart,
32
peas: chicken pie with ham and, 100–1
green leaf and pea soup, 120
peas with leeks, 166
risotto verde, 20
pecan nuts: maple syrup and pecan
muffins, 67
peppers: beef with prunes and, 160
muffleta, 54–5
preserved roasted peppers with basil,
177

Thai stir-fried beef with red peppers,
158
pesto: classic basil, 217
pesto scones, 90
pickle, cucumber, 174
pies: chicken pie with bacon and peas, 100
ham and egg pie, 64
pilaf, chicken, 153
pilaf rice, 218
plums: nectarine, berry and plum
smoothie, 75
rhubarb, plum and cardamom crumble,
169
popcorn paradise, 146
pork: homemade pork sausages, 196–8
pork chops with caramelized apples,
202
Thai pork with coconut cilantro sauce,
156–7
porter cake, 41
potatoes: baked potatoes, 136–8
colcannon, 196–8
garlic and mustard potatoes, 167
potato, chorizo and feta frittata, 63
raclette, 145
prunes, beef with peppers and, 160

quesadillas, 76

raclette, 145
raisins: porter cake, 41
raita, cilantro and lime, 143
raspberries: nectarine, berry and plum
smoothie, 75
red currant jelly, 217
relishes: onion marmalade, 181
spiced cranberry and orange relish, 180
tomato, ginger and chile jam, 178
rhubarb: rhubarb and ginger jam, 185
rhubarb and ginger muffins, 15
rhubarb, plum and cardamom crumble,
169
sponge cake with rhubarb cream, 50
upside-down rhubarb and ginger cake,
28
rice, 218–19
oven-baked risotto, 206
risotto verde, 20
roux, 215

salads: arugula, tomato and sugar snap
pea, 59
avocado, orange and watercress, 123
crab and avocado, 123
crispy bacon, tomato and arugula,
116–17
duck, lentil and red cabbage, 60
green salad with honey mustard
dressing, 150
Vietnamese crab salad, 162
walnut salad, 203
warm pasta salad with herbs, garlic and
arugula, 124
white beans with tomatoes and tuna, 59
salmon: roast Southeast Asian salmon,
161
smoked salmon with baked potatoes, 138
spicy salmon cakes, 25

salsas, 99, 139
samosas, lamb, 143
sandwiches *see* bread
sauces: applesauce, 196–8
  chimichurri sauce, 127
  coconut cilantro sauce, 156–7
  crème Anglaise, 221
  fresh tomato sauce, 82–3
  hollandaise sauce, 98
  hot mocha sauce, 111
  mint sauce, 216
  roux, 215
  tomato ketchup, 80
sausages: homemade pork sausages,
  196–8
  party sausages with mustard and honey
    dip, 83
  spicy sausages with cilantro, 198
scones, 90–1
Serrano ham and Manchego cheese, 136
shortbread cookies, whole wheat, 46
shortcrust pastry, 220
shrimp, light coconut broth with, 97
Sicilian pasta, 165
smoked salmon with baked potatoes, 138
smoothies, 75
soups: broccoli soup with Parmesan
    toasts, 19
  chunky Mediterranean pasta soup, 200
  green leaf and pea soup, 120
  light coconut broth with bok choy and
    basil, 97
  spring greens soup, 119
  winter vegetable broth, 94
sour cream cake, 36
South American beef steak, 127
spaghetti *see* pasta
spinach: pasta with bacon, Parmesan
    and, 23
  quesadillas with, 76

sponge cake with rhubarb cream, 50
spring greens soup, 119
steak with blue cheese butter, 203
stock, 215
strawberry daiquiri, 128
sugar syrup, 221
summer fruit jam, 182
summer omelette, 116–17
summer tiramisu, 130
sundae, toffee, 31
sweet pastry, 221
sweet scones, 91
syrup, sugar, 221

tagine, Moroccan lamb, 154
tarts: asparagus and scallion tart, 61
  chocolate and hazelnut toffee tart, 109
  custard tart, 131
  ham and egg pie, 64
  jam tarts, 68
  no-pastry pear and almond tart, 32
  onion and blue cheese tart, 118
Thai pork, 156–7
Thai rice, 219
Thai stir-fried beef, 158
tiramisu, summer, 130
toffee: butterscotch, 191
  toffee, apple and almond crumble, 170
  toffee popcorn, 146
  toffee sundae, 31
tomatoes: arugula, tomato and sugar
    snap pea salad, 59
  chunky Mediterranean pasta soup, 200
  classic spaghetti and meatballs with
    fresh tomato sauce, 82–3
  creamy pasta with sun-dried tomatoes,
    olives and pine nuts, 24
  creamy tomatoes on toast, 144
  crispy bacon, tomato and arugula salad,
    116–17

gratin of fish with cheese, tomatoes and
    herbs, 106
  pasta with tomato and ginger salsa, 99
  salad of white beans with tuna and, 59
  scrambled eggs with tomato, chile and
    cilantro, 12
  spaghetti with beef, olives, capers and
    anchovies, 105
  spicy tomato and apple chutney, 179
  tomato and cucumber salsa, 139
  tomato, ginger and chile jam, 178
  tomato ketchup, 80
tortillas: quesadillas, 76
truffles, chocolate praline, 189
tuna, salad of white beans with tomatoes
    and, 59

vanilla fudge, 190
vanilla melting moments, 192
vegetable broth, winter, 94
Vietnamese crab salad, 162
vin chaud, 210

walnut salad, 203
watercress: avocado, orange and
    watercress salad, 123
  green leaf and pea soup, 120
white beans: salad with tomatoes and
    tuna, 59
  winter vegetable broth with, 94
white soda scones, 90
whole wheat shortbread cookies, 46
wine: vin chaud, 210
winter vegetable broth, 94

yogurt: lemon and ginger ice cream, 171
  smoothies, 75
  yogurt with oats and honey, 72

ACKNOWLEDGMENTS

I would like to thank all my lovely family and friends for their undying support.

A huge thank you goes to my amazing agents at Limelight Management, Fiona Lindsay and Linda Shanks, and also to Mary Bekhait.

At Collins, Jenny Heller and Emma Callery got me through months of writing, with constant encouraging and cajoling (not to mention bringing a whole new meaning to the word *patience*).

A big thanks, too, for the gorgeous photography to Peter Cassidy and Cristian Barnett, assisted by Claire Davies; to Felicity Barnum-Bobb for her glorious food styling; to Jim, Emma, Katrin, Saskia and Alex at Smith & Gilmour for their beautiful book design; and to Emma Ewbank for designing the lovely cover. Thank you also to Alastair Laing, Kerenza Swift, Iona Murray and makeup artist Liz McCarthy.

Enormous gratitude also to David Hare, Brian Walsh, Billy Keady, Ray de Brún, Anna Ní Mhaonaigh, Emma Brennan, Sally Walker, Neil McLaughlan, Kevin Lavelle, Shermin Mustafa and Caragh Thompson, without whom the filming of the series would not have happened. A very big thanks as well to Beth and Gerry Cuddigan for lending us their lovely house to live in while our own home was being turned into a studio for filming!

Finally, thank you to our lovely friends who came and happily drank and ate with us for the book photos: Lucy, Jasper, Helena, Francesca and Max Wight and Thomas Smiddy.